MEMPHIS STATE UNIVERSITY PRESS

This is copy 251 of a limited edition

Thomas G. Webb
AUTHOR

Tennessee County History Series

TENNESSEE COUNTY HISTORY SERIES

DeKalb County

by Thomas G. Webb

Robert B. Jones
Editor

MEMPHIS STATE UNIVERSITY PRESS

Memphis, Tennessee

Maps prepared by Reaves & Sweeney, Inc., Memphis, Tennessee

Manufactured in the United States of America

Designed by Gary G. Gore

ISBN 0-87870-114-1

Preface

I began collecting material for a history of DeKalb County almost 40 years ago, when I was still in high school. Several years ago Memphis State University Press requested that I write a brief history for the Tennessee County History Series, and this book is the result. Because of the limited length I could not give more than a summary of the county's history. Many interesting anecdotes and many deserving people have had to be omitted, as there was space for little more than the highlights of the past 200 years.

I offer my apologies for the mistakes in the book. Despite all efforts to avoid them, errors are inevitable in a book which contains so many names, dates, and places. I will appreciate your informing me of such mistakes so that they can be corrected in the future.

I wish to express my deepest appreciation to all the people who have been kind and patient enough to tell me about the things they remembered from the past. It would be impossible to name the hundreds with whom I have talked, but I particularly recall Mr. Brown Foster, Mrs. Mattie Cheatham, and Mr. Luther Fuson, to all of whom I went time after time: Mr. and Mrs. Jim Lee of Dallas, Texas, and Mrs. Valerie Burton Lounsbury of Miami, Florida, were dedicated correspondents who wrote page after page of valuable historical material in their many letters.

I also appreciate the many people who have so generously let me borrow their historical pictures, with special thanks to Bundy Bratten and Randall Adcock for making pictures for me in many out-of-the-way places.

I hope that this book will reawaken memories in older people and will make younger people aware of how life was lived in DeKalb County in the past two centuries.

DEDICATION
To the citizens of DeKalb County—
past, present, and future

$\mathcal{D}$EKALB County, Tennessee, was established in December of 1837 by an act of the Tennessee Legislature. The county contains 317 square miles; it is between 25 and 30 miles wide from east to west and slightly less from north to south. With approximately 14,000 people within its boundaries, it is a comparatively small county in both area and population.

The southern part of the county is on a plateau, the Highland Rim, known locally as "the flatwoods." Here great level fields of soybeans and corn are harvested by huge combines and air-conditioned tractors. Smaller patches of tobacco are interspersed with fields of evergreens and fruit trees to give an air of prosperity to the area. It was not always so.

When Riley Turner moved to the flatwoods from the Caney Fork in 1890 his uncle Marion Love visited him, looked around, and said, "You'll never be able to raise your children here." The flatwoods did look discouraging then. They were usually burned off every few years, so that much of the land had only a few big trees mixed with head-high bushes. Corn did well to grow shoulder high and to produce a small nubbin or two. Most of the widely scattered houses were small and unpainted and had stick-and-dirt chimneys. When Zachariah Davis moved to Shiney Rock from Smith Fork in 1884 the house he bought from Jerome Mangum

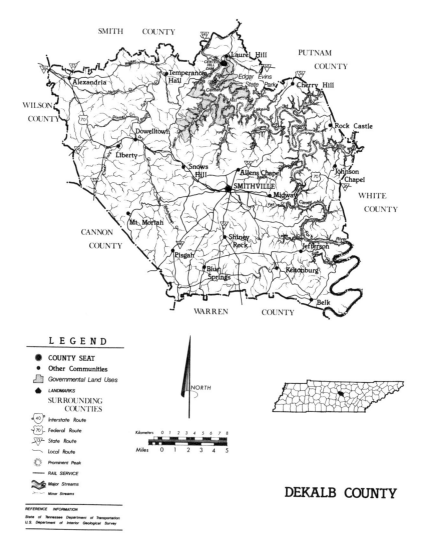

SMITH COUNTY

PUTNAM COUNTY

Laurel Hill

Edgar Evins
State Park

Cherry Hill

Rock Castle

Temperance
Hall

Alexandria

WILSON
COUNTY

Dowelltown

Liberty

Snows
Hill

Allens Chapel

Johnson
Chapel

SMITHVILLE

Midway

WHITE
COUNTY

Mt. Moriah

CANNON
COUNTY

Shiney
Rock

Jefferson

Pisgah

Blue
Springs

Keltonburg

Belk

WARREN   COUNTY

L E G E N D

● COUNTY SEAT
● Other Communities
▱ Governmental Land Uses
◆ LANDMARKS
SURROUNDING
COUNTIES
40 Interstate Route
70 Federal Route
17 State Route
Local Route
Prominent Peak
RAIL SERVICE
Major Streams
Minor Streams

NORTH

Kilometers 0 1 2 3 4 5 6 7 8
Miles   0   1   2   3   4   5

REFERENCE INFORMATION
State of Tennessee Department of Transportation
U.S. Department of Interior Geological Survey

DEKALB COUNTY

had such a chimney, much to the horror of his 11-year-old daughter Nola, who had never before seen one. She had already cried half the day because she saw some of that spindly corn when they passed Tom Cope's place, and she was certain that the whole family would starve.

To the north and east the flatwoods break off sharply to steep hills and hollows leading down to the beautiful blue green waters of Center Hill Lake. Here until 35 years ago the Caney Fork River twisted and looped its way between steep hills and towering gray limestone bluffs, its rich bottom lands producing 100 bushels of corn to the acre year after year without fertilizer.

The western section of the county, in the Smith Fork valley, was about as fertile as the Caney Fork area. In both places there were prosperous farms with large barns and big white houses with wide porches. Here lived the gracious people who could invite friends home from church to eat dinner. Things were less prosperous out on the ridges and far up the steep hollows where cedars grew thick on the limestone rocks. Here it was hard to grow even a small crop of corn, and the best way to make money from it was to make it into whiskey. Quite a few people were engaged in this business, even though all making, selling, and drinking of whiskey was illegal after 1909 in Tennessee.

During most of DeKalb County's first century the people of the Caney Fork and Smith Fork had both more time and more money to spend on education, clothes, houses, horses, etc. than did the people of the flatwoods. It might be expected that some would consider themselves superior to those who lived in the flatwoods section. This naturally led to feelings of resentment; from the beginning there has been, and still is to some extent, a feeling of antagonism between "Under-the-Hill" (as the Liberty-Alexandria area is known) and the Smithville area. This antagonism was increased by political division and especially by the Civil War. In the last two decades, however, it has decreased to a considerable degree.

The geography of DeKalb County has in many ways shaped the lives and destinies of its people. It determined how much money they had, how much education they had, who they vis-

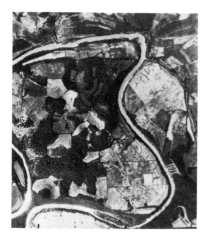

This 1937 aerial view of the Caney Fork River does not show the tall bluffs and steep hollows around the river, but it does show the Narrows, where a man could stand and throw a rock into the river on either side. A boat had to travel six miles around to get from one side to the other.

ited, where they went to church, when and where they traveled. The saying was, "We'll see you if the good Lord's willing and the creeks don't rise." The creeks did rise, however, on many occasions, and when they did, many people had to stay at home. At a number of places in the Smith Fork and Caney Fork areas the road simply ran down the creek bed. This was true for a mile or more on Long Branch, for instance, as late as the 1950s, even though it was the most direct road from Smithville to Center Hill Dam. In such a situation not only did people have to stay at home if the creeks rose, but sometimes they got caught out when they had gone somewhere. About 1925 a large group from the head of Dry Creek went fishing on Smith Fork. On their return trip, their cars got stalled in Dry Creek at the first ford above Dowelltown because there had been a cloudburst on upper Dry Creek. Logs and treetops floated by as the water kept rising. Mrs. Floice Vickers and her sister-in-law were trapped in the back seat of one car, but someone waded in and rescued them; Floice finally backed the car out of the creek. At least sixteen of the group spent that night with Willie Vandergriff, with the women "bedded down on the floor like sweet potatoes."

Roads in the Caney Fork area were even more difficult to build than in other parts of the county because of the size of the river and the steepness of the bluffs and hills. Much of the travel in this area was by horseback and by foot, as there were still no automobile roads in many parts of the Caney Fork region in 1948 when it was covered by the waters of Center Hill Lake. When James Webb taught the one-teacher school at Williams' Cross-roads in 1945 he had to walk out when he wanted to come home to Smithville for the weekend. Then on Sunday afternoon his father drove him across Sligo and up the hill to the Laurel School, from which he walked down the ridge to the Falling Water, which he crossed on a swinging bridge. From there he walked up the hill and around the ridge to his boarding place at Mrs. Daisy Lafever's, a distance of about six miles.

While the physical features of DeKalb County were in some ways a handicap, they provided scenery of unsurpassed beauty. Those who lived in even the poorest of houses without a single picture on the walls had only to step outside or walk a short distance to have a view equal to the finest scenic paintings. Such scenery has been a continuous source of pleasure and enrichment to the citizens of the county.

The climate of DeKalb County is generally moderate, with relatively mild winters and warm summers. Each winter usually has three or four snows, with January and February weather cold enough to freeze the ponds. Summer temperatures seldom reach 100 degrees, and rainfall averages 40 to 50 inches in a normal year.

Normal years, of course, are not the ones that are remembered; the abnormal ones are the memorable ones. The very earliest settlers were faced with drought; in 1800 there was little or no rain from June 15 to November 5. Other hot, dry summers came in 1830, 1881, 1936, 1952, and 1980. The worst of these was 1881, when practically no corn crop was made and thousands of sheep, hogs, and other livestock literally starved to death.

In contrast to these hot summers were the bitter cold winters of 1843, 1884, 1918, 1940, and 1977. The longest period of sustained cold probably came in 1977, when temperatures in January never went above the freezing mark. The ground froze more than two feet deep, and many water pipes were frozen in the ground for two months or more.

Even more destructive than the hot or cold weather were the floods and tornadoes, most of which came during the spring season. On April 23, 1878, there was a tremendous storm which was not a tornado, but which blew down vast amounts of timber all over DeKalb County. Tornadoes have struck various parts of the county; on January 24, 1928, one destroyed the Hayes School on Holmes' Creek, killing four children and injuring the teacher, Grady Carter. On April 3, 1974, a tornado in the western part of the county killed one person before destroying a large part of Dowelltown.

Floods have also been very destructive. On Dry Creek and Smith Fork they damaged and destroyed homes, barns, and fences. The home and mill of Adam Dale, DeKalb's first settler, were wrecked by flood waters before the Civil War; Bates' Mill near the mouth of Walker's Creek was destroyed in the 1902 flood. The Caney Fork River was larger than Smith Fork, and even more destructive. The major floods on the Caney Fork came in 1852, 1902, 1928, and 1929. Although the flood of 1902 washed away many houses and barns, the 1929 flood was much more damaging. Besides the damage on the Caney Fork, the backwaters also flooded the creeks and hollows and floated away buildings and livestock in the entire area. Periodic floods on the Caney Fork were ended in 1948 when Center Hill Reservoir flooded the Caney Fork Valley permanently.

American Indian Inhabitants

The present people of DeKalb County and their ancestors have lived here less than 200 years. This is a comparatively short time in the history of human habitation in the county, as archaeologists believe that men first came to this area during the last Ice Age, about 15,000 years ago. Though no one was living here in 1797 when the first settlement was made, there is evidence of several Indian villages in DeKalb County before A.D. 1500. This evidence consists principally of arrowheads and spearpoints, a few mound sites and some graves, along with one brief archaeological survey made in 1947 of the area now covered by Center Hill Lake. Because of the lack of real research, it has not been possible to give complete information on DeKalb County's first people. However, certain conclusions can be reached.

The first men to come here thousands of years ago were very likely wandering hunters who found the Highland Rim a favorable spot to hunt buffalo and other game. It was then almost prairielike, with long grass and few trees. Animals were apparently attracted to the cold spring at the head of Pine Creek, as many arrowheads and spearpoints have been found there. Many of these are of the period around 2000 to 8000 years ago called the Archaic Era. During that time it is likely that the people lived near a stream, as clams and mussels were among their chief foods. Drills and scrapers of this time have been found on Smith Fork and Clear Fork, indicating a more settled life than the early hunters had. Most Tennessee Indians of this period lived in villages, and most died in their 20s and 30s; few lived to be 50 years old. Like people today many of them suffered from arthritis and abcessed teeth. They had no horses, cows, pigs, or even cats, but they did have dogs, which they evidently valued highly, as they were often buried in the same grave with a person. The only scientific evaluation of Indian occupation of DeKalb County was made in 1947 by the Smithsonian Institution. In a survey of the area to be covered by Center Hill Reservoir they found three large temple mounds, three small earth-rock mounds, three occupied caves, and 28 village sites, all in the comparatively small area of 23,000 acres. At least four of the villages were thought to be at least 2,000 years old: one near Center Hill School, one on Holmes' Creek, one near Sligo, and one at Young Bend. The mouth of Mine Lick Creek seems to have been one of the Indians' favorite spots, as the excavation indicated that it had been occupied almost continuously from about 2000 years ago until about A.D. 1500. At the site were an earth-rock mound, two villages, a burial cave, and a temple mound. This temple mound was about ten feet high, with a rectangular flat top and sloping sides, and was probably built about A.D. 1000–1200. Such temples usually had carved and painted wooden pillars and were hung with colorful mats. The ceremonies in them centered around the planting and harvesting of corn, the chief crop.

There is a large mound on the farm of William Truitt on Smith Fork, but no scientific excavations have been made in the area. Many Indian graves of the Temple Mound era, however, have been found on Smith Fork. They are rock-lined, square, and contain skeletons in a sitting posture. Though we cannot know definitely, it is likely that the life of these people in DeKalb County was similar to that of other people in Tennessee at that time. They were great hunters, and deer furnished the largest part of their meat, though they also ate turkey, bear, squirrel, and rabbit. They played a relatively mild game called chunkey, and a relatively wild game similar to modern lacrosse, which often resulted in broken arms and legs. Among many groups it was customary for every man, woman, and child to submerge in a river four times first thing in the morning, even in the winter. Life was hard for these people, and few of them survived even to middle age.

Before A.D. 1500 the native American Indians in DeKalb County and Middle Tennessee had a flourishing civilization; yet when the first European settlers came to the area there were no Indian tribes living in Middle Tennessee. It was used as a hunting ground by several tribes, especially the Cherokees. It was they and the Creeks who fought against the settlement of Middle Tennessee from 1779 to 1794. In 1789 James Winchester, a military leader of Sumner County, and a scouting party fought a skirmish with a group of Cherokees near the junction of Clear Fork and Smith Fork. One of Winchester's men was killed, as was one Indian, a hare-lipped warrior named Moon. On another occasion a group of 30 men under a Lieutenant Snoddy of Sumner County pursued some Indians up the Caney Fork to their camp at Rock Island. There they fought a battle and the Indians were driven away. This was in November 1793; four years later Adam Dale became the first white settler in what would become DeKalb County.

First European Settlement

The first European explorers of the DeKalb County area were hunters, and certainly there was much for them to hunt; DeKalb County's woods and canebrakes were filled with game. In the winter of 1780 some 20 of the first settlers of Nashville made a hunting trip up the Caney Fork in canoes. They returned with 105 bears, 75 buffalo, and 80 deer. Before the actual settlement of the county a group of hunters, which included William King and William Terril, had a hunting camp on Mine Lick Creek. Hunting had its dangers, especially while the Indians still roamed the area. In 1793 James Randal Robertson and John Grimes had been killed by the Cherokees "on the waters of the Caney Fork, where they had gone to trap for beaver." But the Indian raids ended in 1794 after the Nickajack expedition wiped out a large number of the most aggressive warriors. With Middle Tennessee apparently safe from the terrors of Indian warfare, settlement began to spread out farther from the forts and stations where it had been centered.

Adam Dale was the first to settle permanently in what is now DeKalb County. He probably explored the area in 1797 and returned to Nashville. The next year he came back with Stephen Robinson and two brothers, Leonard and John Fite, who brought the first wagon into the Smith Fork Valley. These men, like most early settlers, were looking for good land. They were not, however, penniless wanderers; all four of them were settled family men, and all were relatively prosperous.

It was good that they were prosperous; otherwise they could not have acquired any land. We now visualize the pioneer exploring the wilderness, building his log cabin, and staking out his claim. That is not the way things were in DeKalb County, however, for practically all the best land had been claimed by speculators years before the actual settlers arrived. Much of DeKalb County lay within the reservation that North Carolina had set aside for its Revolutionary War soldiers. Practically all the soldiers sold their claims to wealthy speculators, however, preferring what money they could get in hand to the unknown

Adam Dale (*left*) at about 80 years old of age (from *DeKalb County History*, opposite page 24). Revolutionary War veteran Ebenezer Snow used this cave (*right*) to stable his horses.

acres across the mountains. The speculator, of course, took a considerable chance, and often it was many years before he got any return from his money. Speculators owned all the best land on Smith Fork, Dry Creek, Clear Fork, and the Caney Fork. Much of Dry Creek and upper Smith Fork was owned by John and Stockley Donelson, the father and brother of Mrs. Andrew Jackson, and Adam Dale bought his 320 acres at Liberty from Robert Hayes, Mrs. Jackson's brother-in-law. Thomas Stokes of North Carolina owned 4000 acres on Smith Fork, from above Helton Creek to below Walker's Creek. On the Caney Fork, much of the land was owned by the Davis family of Pasquetonk County, North Carolina.

By the time the state of Tennessee began to sell grants of land in 1806 most of the good land was gone. Little was left in DeKalb County except hill land and the flatwoods, and most of that was not considered worth $2.00 an acre, the price charged by the state. Consequently, grants made by the state before 1820 in DeKalb County were generally small, less than 100 acres, and some were only 15 or 20 acres.

The land for sale in DeKalb County was not attractive to people who were really poor. Adam Dale, for example, came from a family of some property. His grandfather, John Dale of Worcester County, Maryland, owned eight slaves and a plantation, as well as a silver watch and a copper still, all of which he left to Adam Dale's father, Thomas. When Thomas Dale died in 1812 near Liberty, Tennessee, his estate included not only land and slaves, but books, maps, pictures, a cut and engraved decanter, and a curtain bedstead.

Stephen Robinson, the first settler at Temperance Hall, owned land and slaves in Cumberland County, Virginia, as early as 1783. When he made his will in 1828, he owned 14 slaves and more than 1000 acres of land. John and Leonard Fite, who also came to DeKalb County in 1798, were sons of a German immigrant to New Jersey. Their father owned land and a gristmill there, and John and Leonard both prospered in Tennessee. Leonard Fite by 1820 owned nine slaves, a mill, and 590 acres at the present site of Dowelltown. Daniel Alexander, born in 1773 in Maryland, founded the town of Alexandria on his land in 1820. By that year he owned 10 slaves, but he evidently had a substantial house built by 1802, when he was licensed to keep a tavern at his dwelling.

Not all the early settlers were as prosperous as these mentioned, but almost all were of a fairly substantial background. They could buy at least a few acres, build a log house, grow enough to eat and wear, and have a considerable measure of independence.

By 1820 there were about 2000 people living in what is now DeKalb County. At least half of them lived on Dry Creek, Clear Fork, and Smith Fork and its tributaries. About seventy families were scattered around the Caney Fork and its tributaries. A few more families lived around Belk, and on Sink, Pine, and Fall creeks. Much of the flatwoods had no people at all; the area south of present Highway 70 through Crossroads to Sink Creek was virtually unpopulated for most of a century. Even in the areas with more people, the farms were separated by great stretches of woods. Wolves and wildcats prowled through them, and even bears were a threat to livestock during the early years of settlement. Though the wolves and bears have been gone for many years, wildcats are still occasionally seen in the county.

Few of DeKalb County's settlers were born in foreign countries; most of the families had been in America for three or four generations. About three-fourths of DeKalb Countians are of English origin; the remainder are mainly Scotch and Irish, with some German, Dutch, and French, and a few Swiss and Scandinavians. The DeKalb Countians of African origin, like the ones of European origin, had apparently been in America for three or four generations before coming to DeKalb County.

The pattern of migration to DeKalb County can be seen in the travels of the Cantrell family. Richard Cantrell of Derbyshire, England, was in Philadelphia by 1689. His son moved to Delaware; his grandson to North Carolina. From there the family spread into South Carolina, and by 1801 into the DeKalb County area of Tennessee. Several more Cantrells moved to Tennessee during the next 30 years, but even before they could all arrive from the Carolinas, some of the first ones were moving on to Illinois, Missouri, and Texas. However, enough remained in DeKalb County to make Cantrell the most common name in the county today.

The next most numerous family, the Taylors, followed a similar pattern. From Virginia, they moved to North Carolina and then to Elbert County, Georgia, before settling on Indian Creek in DeKalb County about 1806. Within twenty years they too were moving to other states—Indiana, Illinois, Arkansas, and Texas. However, like the Cantrells, enough Taylors remained in DeKalb County to produce a very large family.

Though they were not as numerous as the Cantrells and Taylors, most DeKalb County families followed similar patterns of migration. The vast majority came from North Carolina, South Carolina, and Virginia, with a few from Delaware, Maryland, Kentucky, and Georgia. Very few came from New England or other states.

Some Known Settlers in DeKalb County, 1797–1820

Liberty: Mathias Anderson; William Anderson; Cantrell Bethel and his brother Larkin; James Bratten; Richard Cantrell; Adam Dale and his brothers Isaac, Thomas, Jr., and William; Thomas Donnell; Josiah Duncan; Joseph Evans; Walter Evans; George Givan and his brother William; Lawrence Lamberson; William P. Lawrence; Robert W. Roberts; and Anthony Walke

Alexandria Area: Daniel Alexander, Giles Bowers, David Coffee, Joshua Coffee, Stewart Doss, Patrick McEachern, David Vantrease

Temperance Hall Area: Isaac Bates, Nathaniel Corley, Robert Corley, Burrell Driver, Bowling Felts, Conrad Lamberson, Thomas Pistole, Stephen Robinson

Hannah's Branch: John Davis, William Lawrence, James Tubb, Jr.

Lower Smith Fork: Abner Avant, Giles Driver, Jacob Overall, Gay Reynolds and his brothers James, John, and Josiah

Helton Creek and Walker's Creek: Elijah Ditter, William Field, Elijah Foutch, Jonathan Foutch, William Foutch, James Goodner, Abraham Hass, James Malone, Robert Malone, William Malone, Luke McDowell, John West, Thomas West, and William Thweatt

Dismal Creek: Benjamin Bennett, John Bennett, Richard Bennett, William Bennett, Jonathan Griffith, John Hicks, Reuben Johnson, Solomon Scott, Peter Vanatta, Samuel Vanatta, and Rebecca Yeargin

Lower Dry Creek: George Barnes, William Bratten, Leonard Fite, Aaron Frazier, Howard Gray, Matthew Griffin, Thomas Hart, Henry Hays, James Hays, Jesse Mann, Phillip Payne, Benjamin Snow and his brother Joseph, William Williams, Sr., and his sons Gilbert, Samuel, and William, Jr.

Upper Dry Creek: Aaron Braswell, Sampson Braswell, Peter Etheridge, Joseph Graham, William Johnstone, Cooper Melton, Matthew Melton, Thomas Melton, Archibald Sellars, Drury Sellars, John Sellars, Jordan Sellars, Ebenezer Snow and his son William, Matthew Spurlock, and Moses Wilder

Clear Fork: Abraham Adams, Jacob Adams, John Adamson, William Adamson, Daniel Allen, Thomas Dale, Sr., William Goggin, John Looney, Abraham Overall, George Turney, Isaac Turney, Jacob Turney, James Turney, and Thomas Whaley

Upper Smith Fork: John Allen, Lewis Allen, Moses Allen, Samuel Bethel, Silas Cooper, John Crips, John Estes, Moses Estes and his brother William, John Fite, Ephraim Garrison, Jesse Garrison, Moses Garrison, Nehemiah Garrison, Samuel Garrison, Charles Hays, John Hays, Peter Ruyle, Bird Spurlock, and William Truitt

Lower Caney Fork: Archibald Braswell, John Den, William Love, William Rafferty, Andrew Starnes, John Tibbs

Cove Hollow: John Blanton; John Dill; Joseph Dill, Sr., and his son Joseph, Jr.; William Dill, Sr., and his son William, Jr.; Joab Hale, George Robinson

Indian Creek: James Hendrixson; Jonathan Hendrixson; Archibald McIntire; Abner Self; Barzela, Benjamin, David, Drury, Henry, John, and William Taylor (all of whom were related); and William Tramel

Holmes' Creek: Hezekiah Allen, John Brownfield, Joel Cheatham, Benjamin Clark, Isaac Hayes, Richard McGinnis, Thomas Megginson, Bartemus Pack, William Pack, Barnabas Page and his brother Jacob, Shadrack Phillips, John Williams, Jonathan Wiseman, and Thomas Wood

Middle Caney Fork: George Allen and his brothers Jesse and Samuel Hunt Allen, Peter Billings, John Heath, Zachariah LeFevre, Matthew Martin, John Parsley, Moses Pedigo, John Puckett, and Micajah Rackley

Upper Caney Fork: Aaron Cantrell, Richard Crowder, William Erwin, James Ferguson, John Hibdon, Edward Hooper, Allen Johnson, Brittain Johnson, Micajah Johnson, John Kelley, Drury Maynard, James McClarn, Anthony Pate, John Pate, and Richard Porterfield

Mine Lick Creek: Henry Burton; David Herrin, Sr., and his son David, Jr.; William Herrin; Molliston Pettyjohn

Falling Water River: Levi Bozarth, James Davis, James Dildine, George W. Eastham, Giles Elrod, James Elrod, John Robinson, and Archibald Warren

Belk Area: Simon Adamson, John Dunham, William Dunham, John Fisher, Joseph Franks, Elijah Hooten, and Joseph Rankhorn

Sink Creek: David, Isaac, Leonard, and William Adcock (all of whom were related); Harmon Banks; Elizabeth Beshearse; Abraham, Benjamin, Hardin, James, John, Richard, Sampson, and Watson Cantrell (all of whom were related); Mark Forrest; Joseph Jadwin; Hardy Johnson; Elizabeth Kirby; John Linder; Perry Green Magness; John Martin; George Payne; and Tilman Potter

Pine Creek: Thomas Cantrell; Thomas Durham; Abraham Farrington; Elijah Gorman; George Gorman; William Howard, Sr.; William Paine; Harmon Redmon and his son Solomon; and James Young and his brother John

Fall Creek: John Cannady (Kennedy) and his sons James and John, Abraham Cantrell, James Colwell, Giles Driver, Reddick Driver, and James Lockhart

Allen's Ferry Road: Thomas Bradford, John Frazier, Joseph Frazier, Levi Frazier, Edmund League, John Martin, Tavner Martin and his son Zachariah.

Early Days in DeKalb County

DeKalb County was established in December of 1837 from parts of Warren, White, Cannon, and Jackson counties. However, Cannon County had been established only in 1836, and very little of Jackson County was included in DeKalb. For most of the forty years between its first settlement in 1797 and its establishment as a county DeKalb County was a part of Smith, Warren, and White counties. Alexandria, Liberty, and Temperance Hall were in Smith County. The line between Smith and Warren counties cut across Holmes' Creek, Snow's Hill, and Dry Creek. Most of the flatwoods area and east to the Caney Fork was in Warren County, including present Smithville. East of the Caney Fork from Little Hurricane to Rock Island was in White County before 1837. The original boundaries of the county have been altered to some extent; in 1854 a large section on the northeast corner was given to Putnam County. In 1852 and 1854 sections were taken from Smith County and added to DeKalb, including Walker's Creek, part of Temperance Hall, and Wolf Creek. Since that time the county's boundaries have changed very little.

DeKalb County was named by the Tennessee legislature in honor of Johann DeKalb, who was born in Germany in 1721. He served as a major general during the American Revolution and died at Camden, North Carolina, in 1780 after being wounded in battle. The legislature also specified that the county seat should be named Smithville, in honor of Samuel Granville Smith who had died in 1835. He had served as the first mayor of Gainesboro, as a state senator, and was Tennessee's secretary of state at the time of his death.

The geographical center of the new county was found to be about a mile northwest of the present courthouse at what is now the Kennedy Cemetery. Since Bernard Richardson offered to donate 50 acres at the present site of Smithville this site was selected. The first court met in March of 1838 at Mr. Richardson's log home on the bank of Fall Creek just east of the town site; they continued to meet there for more than a year.

The 50-acre site of Smithville was divided into 92 lots separated by streets and alleys, with a public square in the center, where construction was soon begun on the courthouse. A two-story brick jail was built on the corner of Main and College streets, a block west of the square, and the court met there in October of 1839. In July of 1840 the court met in the completed courthouse, a brick building with four offices on the main floor and a large courtroom on the second floor. This first courthouse stood north of the center of the square and had a fence around it to keep out roaming livestock.

The second courthouse, built in 1890, was in the center of the square and had no fence around it. This was an unfortunate omission, as hogs found the hall of the courthouse a convenient sleeping place, especially in the winter. The stairs to the second

There are several spectacular falls where the streams drop from the Highland Rim into the Central Basin. This is Culcarmac Falls on Fall Creek two miles below Smithville. It was a favorite spot for young couples on May rambles around 1900.

floor were often used as a roosting spot by the geese of Mrs. Scott Tyree, who lived near the square.

The second courthouse was not built just to house the town's livestock, however, but to replace the badly deteriorated first courthouse. The first jail was replaced at the same time. A countywide referendum was held at that time on a plan to move the county seat to a location between Liberty and Dowelltown, but it failed to pass. The new jail, a brick building with three cells, was built on the south side of the square and had five rooms for the sheriff and his family. It became customary at this time for the sheriff to live at the jail rather than to hire a jailer. The second jail was destroyed by fire, and the present brick jail was built to replace it in 1959.

The second courthouse was also destroyed by fire. In a spectacular blaze in 1925 the almost-new General Stores building on the south side of the square burned to the ground. Sparks from that fire caught in birdnests in the courthouse cupola, and the courthouse also burned to the ground. Fortunately, most of the record books were rescued. A new fireproof concrete, steel, and brick courthouse was built in 1925 and remained in use until it was torn down in 1970 to be replaced by the present steel and granite structure, a Model Cities project.

Until recent years, the county officials found it necessary to live in Smithville during their terms of office. The county officials have been generally honest and efficient, though sometimes rather casual in their conduct of the affairs of their offices. For instance, in 1925 the state auditor reported that he could not audit the previous trustee as he had the books at his home fifteen miles from the county seat; "the present trustee has his office in a grocery store," and as to the county court clerk who had just left office, "the records as kept by him are so vague that it is impossible to make a satisfactory audit of the office." A much more businesslike atmosphere is maintained by the present county officials.

Participants in Early Wars

There was no DeKalb County when the American Revolution was fought, but several veterans of that war settled in DeKalb County. In fact, the first settler, Adam Dale, had served in the Revolution in Maryland when only fifteen years old; his father, Thomas Dale, was a lieutenant in that war. Other very early settlers who served in the Revolution were John and Leonard Fite of New Jersey, John Puckett and Edmund League of Virginia, and Thomas West and Ebenezer Snow of Delaware. Later settlers who were also veterans of the revolutionary war were John Fisher, Elijah Hooten, and Joseph Rankhorn, all of the Belk vicinity; John Christian of Temperance Hall; Lawrence Lamberson of Liberty; Phillip Palmer of Alexandria; Elijah Duncan and James Saunders near Clear Fork; John Bevert near Smithville; William Childress on the Falling Water; Ruffin Rackley at Second Creek; and William Love near Wolf Creek.

Adam Dale, having served in the Revolution when he was very young, was able also to serve in the War of 1812; he organized a company of mounted gunmen in December of 1813 with himself as captain. Among the 57 men was his 14-year-old son Thomas. Though this company served less than three months, it played an important part in the battle of Emuckfaw Creek in Alabama, where three soldiers of the company were killed and several were wounded. The government paid 40 cents a day for the men's horses, but men were worth less; the privates of the company were paid 25 cents a day. Abraham Overall of Clear Fork, who served as a major in this battle, had a horse killed under him.

In the fall of 1814 at least three more companies were raised in what became DeKalb County. Some of the same people went back again; Jonathan Glover served in Adam Dale's company and in Edward Robinson's company. In fact, Edward Robinson himself served as a private in Dale's company before becoming captain of a company. John Looney and James Tubb were also captains of companies; all three of these companies served for about six months in 1814 and 1815. Edward Robinson's company was at the Battle of New Orleans, while James Tubb's and John Looney's companies were at Pensacola and Mobile.

The companies raised by Dale, Looney, Tubb, and Robinson were principally from the part of DeKalb County that was then in Smith County. The remainder of the county was then in Warren and White Counties and was very sparsely settled at the time. Some of the men in Warren County served in James Tate's company of infantry under Colonel Copeland; they fought with Jackson at the Battle of Horseshoe Bend in Alabama. No doubt other men served in the War of 1812 from these areas, but no other captains or companies have been identified.

The brief Black Hawk War against the Indians in Wisconsin in 1832 had the service of Levi Foutch of Alexandria, and probably that of other DeKalb Countians. Several DeKalb Countians served in the six-year war against the Seminole Indians in Florida, which began in 1836, although no local company was raised.

The Mexican War, which began in 1846, was the first war to occur after DeKalb County was organized. Tennessee was requested to send 2800 men and responded with more than ten times that many, reinforcing her nickname of "Volunteer State," bestowed after her response to the call for volunteers in the War of 1812. Two companies of DeKalb Countians had the privilege of serving in the Mexican War. Captain John F. Goodner of Alexandria raised Company I of the First Tennessee Regiment of Mounted Infantry, and John H. Savage of Smithville organized Company F, Third Regiment of Tennessee Infantry. Captain Goodner's company saw action in the battles of Vera Cruz and Cerro Gordo after a stormy crossing of the Gulf of Mexico, during which part of the horses had to be thrown overboard.

When John H. Savage was promoted to colonel, his brother Abram became captain of that company. This company also had a stormy crossing of the Gulf, with much seasickness. Arriving in Mexico after the major battles had already been fought, Savage's company served as occupation troops until the peace treaty was signed. Due to excessive sickness, however, the company suffered casualties higher than many companies engaged in combat; of a hundred men, seventeen died in less than a year.

The Mexican War served as a training ground for the Civil War 13 years later. Many served in both wars, and some became high-ranking officers. Both John F. Goodner and John H. Savage served as colonels in the Confederate Army, and several other Civil War officers had seen service in the Mexican War.

Home Life, 1800–1860

The shelters of the first settlers were little more than that, but within a few months most of them had built substantial hewn log houses. Many of these were one-room structures with a loft above and a stone chimney. Some had another log room added, with an open hall or "dog-trot" between. A few frame houses were built; Adam Dale's father in 1812 built a two-story frame house on Clear Fork which is still standing. Another house which is still standing was built about 1821 by Samuel Caplinger of Temperance Hall. The house has a stone basement, two full stories, and an attic. Its structure is unlike any other known house in Tennessee; its walls are made of heavy hewn timbers filled with brick, plastered inside and covered outside with clapboard. Only three known brick residences were built in the county before 1900.

This house at Temperance Hall, built in 1821 by Samuel Caplinger, is the only structure in DeKalb County listed on the National Register of Historic Places. It was owned for many years by Nicholas Smith.

The oldest was a two-story structure built around 1801 on Smith Fork by Bowling Felts. The other two were in Alexandria, one of which is still standing. Now owned by Jimmy Mullinax, it was built about 1850 by John B. Yeargin.

The oldest known house still standing in the county is the one built on Clear Fork about 1809 by Abraham Overall. A two-story log structure, it has an unusual plan and features panel doors and wainscoting in the main room. It is now occupied by Colonel Overall's great-grandson, Hoyte Vickers.

Of the houses built in DeKalb County before the Civil War, well over 90 percent were log structures. They were not just temporary cabins, but were substantial homes built to last for years. Even the wealthy lived in log houses; the largest slaveholder in the county was James Tubb, who in 1817 built a log house which still stands on Smith Fork. Cool in summer and warm in winter, log houses were satisfactory in many ways, and they were still being built in DeKalb County as late as 1918.

Furniture was scarce in all houses, especially in the earliest years. The one item which everybody had, and the most valuable of all, was the bed—not the bedstead, but the featherbed itself. Equal to the value of three or four cows, the featherbed was worth twenty times the value of the bedstead. Besides the bed and the corded bedstead, most people had a trunk or a chest for storage, some sort of table, and possibly chairs. However, many early settlers used benches and stools made from hewn logs fitted with legs. Corner cupboards and chests of drawers were common by the 1840s. It was customary for the parents' bedroom to serve as a sitting room for both family and guests, and there was probably not a parlor in the county before 1850. Shortly before the Civil War possibly a dozen or so wealthy families furnished parlors with sofas and padded chairs, but such things were generally rare in DeKalb County.

Equally rare was the kitchen cookstove, which made its appearance just before the Civil War. Prior to that time all cooking was done in the fireplace. This necessarily limited the menu to what could be stewed in the pot, fried in the skillet, or baked in the Dutch oven. Some baking was done in the ashes and occasionally meat was roasted by hanging it in front of the fire. The early settlers ate much wild game, including bear and venison. By 1815, however, hogs were more plentiful and furnished the principal meats for more than a century. Cows were kept mainly to provide milk and butter, and chickens were relatively scarce before the Civil War, probably because there were so many wild animals. Gardens provided beans, peas, squash, cabbage, and pumpkins; tomatoes were thought to be poison and were rarely grown before 1860. Both Irish potatoes and sweet potatoes were being grown by 1850. Cornbread was a main part of every meal, though biscuits made from wheat flour were not unusual by the 1840s. Most food was grown at home, but when William H. Allen died on the Caney Fork in 1841 his widow's provisions for a year included, besides a demijohn of whiskey and 30 killing hogs, 100 pounds of coffee, 200 pounds of brown sugar, 4 loaves of white sugar, 1 pound of tea, 25 pounds of rice, 2 pounds of pepper, 1 pound of ginger, and 4 cakes of chocolate. Coffee was in common use as early as 1806; while cane sugar was scarce in early times, maple sugar was being made by the settlers before 1810.

Like food, clothes were mostly homegrown. Cotton, wool, and flax were grown on the farm, spun on wheels into thread, and woven on looms into cloth before being cut and sewed into garments. Because so much labor was required, people owned very few clothes. Two or three dresses made up the entire wardrobe of the ordinary housewife; many men owned not even one suit. Children wore hand-me-downs as a matter of course, and were glad to get them. Even after "factory cloth" became available in the 1820s, the ordinary family still had very few clothes. There were exceptions, of course. As early as 1814, when John Hays died on upper Smith Fork, he left his son Charles a beaver hat and a suit with "a velvet jacket and breeches." In 1825 Agnes Simpson of Temperance Hall bought three tortoiseshell combs, a pair of silk gloves, and a "straw bonnet with trimmings" which by itself cost as much as a cow and calf. Just before the Civil War Alexandria was noted for having a number of residents who dressed in the latest styles.

Most of the early recreation was also homemade. Much of it centered around work—house-raisings, log-rollings, and corn-shuckings. Men could work hard all day and then dance all night. The women worked hard too; they cooked great mounds of food, washed the dishes and sometimes did some quilting in the afternoon. They, too, were ready for the dance that night. By the 1830s, however, several of the churches had found dancing to be sinful and the fiddle to be the instrument of the devil. Among the more devout church-going families, the dance was replaced by the play-party, which featured singing and marching games, but no dancing and no musical instruments. Among those singing games were "Old Dan Tucker," "Shoot the Buffalo," and "Skip to My Lou." Other games without singing were "Pleased or Displeased" (which survived down almost to the present time) and "Pretty Bird in My Cup." In this game "It" secretly names a bird, then goes to each player carrying a cup containing a wet rag. Each player names a bird, hoping not to name the one "It" has picked, because if he does, the wet rag is thrown in his face and he becomes "It."

Many of the diversions were for males only. In the earliest times all males over 21 were required to be in the militia (similar to today's national guard), and musters were held four times a year. Though it was theoretically a duty, very little military train-

This log house at Young Bend was typical of houses all over DeKalb County before 1860. They served as shelter for rich and poor alike; some are still in use after more than 170 years.

ing occurred, and the women always complained that the muster was just an excuse for the men to get away from home and drink and gamble and fight. Drinking and gambling also went on at the horse races and shooting matches which were popular in the 1830s and 1840s, though these, too, were condemned by the churches. Swimming was an acceptable diversion, though for males only until well after 1900. Church services themselves were social occasions, and camp meetings were great diversions for many who attended. Still, the most popular diversion was centered in the home. This was the social visit. Whole families would drop in to visit the neighbors until bedtime, and young people would visit friends and relatives on weekends or to spend the night. Hospitality was unquestioned in those times of difficult travel, and isolated families welcomed visitors who could bring some variety and perhaps a bit of news into their lives.

Slavery

Slavery existed in DeKalb County from the arrival of the first settlers until the end of the Civil War, although it was not really widespread at any time. Less than one family in six owned slaves, and the average DeKalb County slaveholder owned only three or four. There were no great cotton plantations with dozens of slaves, and in some respects the slaves were treated like members of the family. Though they did plenty of hard work, the slaves usually worked with the owner or with the owner's children. John A. Fite of Alexandria worked beside his father's slaves cutting hay and wheat, plowing, and hoeing. On the Caney Fork, James Koger said that slave owners "worked in the fields with them, I have seen with my own eyes a negro man and his master plowing side by side."

Treatment varied greatly from one owner to another, of course. Mrs. Frances Groom of Liberty, both of whose parents had been slaves, said that they gave very different pictures of slavery. Her mother, who had been owned by Ned Robinson on Smith Fork, reported that they had a good log house, feather pillows, and plenty to eat. The Robinson children worked side by side with the slaves, who were always treated well. Frances' father, George Turner, on the other hand, was owned by a man in Wilson County, and his treatment was quite different. George slept on sacks of hay on planks nailed to the wall and hardly had a decent meal in the years he lived there. When George's brother let the calf get to the cow and take all the milk, he was beaten until he bled. While there is evidence that some slaves in DeKalb County were whipped, there seems to have been very little of such treatment after the slaves passed childhood.

Relations between the slaves and the owner's family were generally good, especially among the younger members of the family. Eli Evans of Liberty recalled visiting his Cousin Tom Vick and going to old Emily's slave cabin "to hear her talk and tell ghost and witch tales." Owners were generally concerned about what became of their slaves after the owners' death. Stephen Robinson's will specified that his slaves should "remain in the family," and James Tubb at his wife's request divided a family of his slaves among his own family. William Goggin in his will stated that black Malinda "for her kindness" was to live with any of his children that she chose.

Unfortunately there were times when the owner could not

control the circumstances. In 1849 a five-year-old girl belonging to George Eastham was sold by the sheriff at the courthouse door for $230 because her owner was in debt. Here was one of the basic tragedies of slavery, the possibility of the separation of families when the children were so young. Slave children as young as three years old were sold in DeKalb County on more than one occasion. Even when slaves were kept by the owner's family, the mother might go to one family member while her child would go to another. When Edward Hooper died in 1838 a slave mother and her child were sold together to the same owner, but the sixty-year-old grandmother was sold to someone else for only $50.

Old slaves had little value, but young ones were always valuable and became more so. Males were generally valued higher than females, and by 1860 an eight-year-old boy was valued at $800. In terms of present-day value, the price of a good slave was about equal to that of an automobile. Actually comparatively little slave trading was carried on in DeKalb County. Slaves never composed more than 10 percent of the population; in some areas there were practically none. Hardly anyone owned slaves in the flatwoods south of Smithville, or on Indian Creek and Holmes' Creek. A few were scattered on the Caney Fork, but the largest numbers were on Smith Fork and around Smithville, Liberty, and Alexandria. In 1850 John Martin near Short Mountain owned 25 slaves; in 1860 James Tubb, John Thomas Stokes, and John Shaw each owned 22. Dabney League and his brother Riley each owned 12, and only a dozen other families owned ten or more slaves.

There was one family of free blacks in the county, that of Elijah Whiteley a few miles north of Smithville. Another free black, Peter Pate, died in 1845 in the Jefferson vicinity. Even free blacks were under certain restrictions, though they were not in as low a social position as slaves. In spite of their inferior status, slaves were accepted into church membership. One of the charter members of Salem Baptist Church in 1809 was a slave , and the congregation continued to accept slaves as members until the Civil War. The Methodist Church in Liberty also had slave members, though they sat in an upstairs gallery apart from the other members.

All in all, slavery in DeKalb County appears to have been no worse than it was in other places; in many ways it was better because the number of slaves was small, and the relationship between slaves and owner was on a very personal basis.

Politics, 1797–1861

The people of DeKalb County have always taken a strong interest in politics and elections. If anything, the interest was stronger in the past than it is today. In a time when there were no ball games or television, political speeches and events furnished much of the entertainment. In antebellum Tennessee governors and local officials were elected every two years on odd years, while elections for United States presidents and congressmen were held on even years, so that some sort of election was being held almost every year. This kept dissension and strife going all the time, for DeKalb County never had any political unity. From the moment of its first organization in 1837 it was almost evenly divided between the two major parties of the time, the Whigs and the Democrats. The residents of the new county tended to follow the pattern of the counties to which they had formerly belonged. Smith County was strongly Whig; so was the Liberty-Alexandria area which had been part of Smith County. Warren County was strongly Democrat, and so was the area around Smithville and south through the flatwoods, which had been part of Warren County. White County was divided between Whigs and Democrats, as was the region around the Caney Fork which was taken from White County to become part of DeKalb. When the three parts of the county were put together, the result was an almost even division between Whigs and Democrats. In the governor's election of 1849 the Democrats carried DeKalb County 592 to 590. However, in 1851 and 1853, the Whigs carried DeKalb, though by less than 25 votes each time.

Such close votes caused DeKalb's citizens to be very strong in their party loyalties. In the 1970s, people used bumper stickers on cars and trucks to show their support for a candidate. As far

John H. Savage was lieutenant colonel of a regiment in the Mexican War. He then served five terms in Congress before being elected colonel of a Confederate regiment.

William B. Stokes served in both the Tennessee General Assembly and the U.S. Congress before becoming a colonel in the Union army during the Civil War (from *DeKalb County History,* opposite page 188).

back as the 1840s supporters of James K. Polk striped their ox-carts and the horns of their oxen with pokeberry juice, while supporters of Henry Clay did the same with clay.

Political campaigns were usually conducted by both candidates traveling together and both speaking at the same gathering. Such gatherings for major candidates were usually held at Alexandria, Liberty, and the Fulton Academy grounds at Smithville; they often lasted three or four hours. Although the political issues were always mentioned, much emphasis was put on entertaining the crowd by telling funny stories and jokes and trying to make the other candidate appear ridiculous. One of the hottest campaigns before the Civil War was the 1859 campaign for U.S. representative. Both candidates were from DeKalb County; the Democrat, John H. Savage of Smithville, was opposed by William B. Stokes of Alexandria. Savage had already served four terms as congressman and had taken advantage of the govern-

ment give-away programs to send many of his constituents pack-
ages of tobacco seed. Unfortunately they turned out to be cabbage
seed instead, and Stokes made great fun of this, referring to Savage as "the cabbage-seed candidate." Savage carried DeKalb
County 825 to 753, but Stokes won the nine-county district by
342 votes.

By 1861 the political issues were much more serious. The big
question was whether or not Tennessee would secede from the
Union. After South Carolina and other states seceded a statewide referendum was held on February 8, 1861, to see if a convention should be called to discuss secession. Tennessee as a whole
voted against the convention by a 55 percent majority. Smith and
Wilson Counties voted strongly against secession, but White and
Warren Counties voted strongly in favor of it. DeKalb County
voted against secession 1009 to 336. The next four months, however, brought events which would change many minds. The most
far-reaching of these came in April after Fort Sumter was fired
on, and President Lincoln called on the states for volunteers to
put down the rebellion. The President's action changed the minds
of many Tennesseans, and when a second referendum was held
on June 8, 1861, the state voted in favor of secession by a two-
to-one margin. Wilson and Smith Counties voted as strongly for
secession as they had voted against it four months earlier. In
Warren County, of more than 1400 voters, all but 12 voted in
favor of secession. In DeKalb County, the vote was also in favor
of secession, but by a much smaller margin than in the surrounding counties. Though 833 voted for secession, 642 voted against
it, meaning that almost half the people of the county were still
loyal to the Union.

Surprisingly enough, slavery seems to have had little to do
with the results of the referendum. The voters of the Alexan-
dria-Liberty-Smith Fork area, where there were many slaves, voted
against secession; residents of the flatwoods, where there were
few slaves, voted in favor of secession. William B. Stokes, who
campaigned strongly against secession, probably had a great influence on the outcome of the referendum in DeKalb County.
And the outcome of the referendum had an even more lasting

influence on the county. Many of those loyal to the Union joined the Federal Army. When they and the Confederates returned home after the Civil War many brought with them an enmity and bitterness which caused political division for more than a century.

The Civil War and Its Aftermath

Though none of the great battles of the Civil War took place in DeKalb County, its citizens experienced greater suffering during that four-year period than during any other period in its history. Partly this was the result of the conflict and the fact that so many men were involved; partly it was the result of the sympathies of DeKalb Countians being divided between the Confederate and Union causes. While in most parts of the South the people were united in fighting against outsiders, in DeKalb County the people were not only fighting outsiders, they were also fighting each other.

In the first months of the war Confederate sentiment seemed to predominate, and all those who first enlisted in the army were Confederates. Nashville was occupied by the Union army on February 24, 1862, however, and within three months William B. Stokes was organizing his regiment of Union cavalry, in which a number of DeKalb Countians served.

During the summer of 1862 both Union and Confederate troops passed through DeKalb County, but the main military action in DeKalb took place during the first six months of 1863. After the Battle of Murfreesboro ended on January 2, 1863, Confederate forces withdrew to Tullahoma and established a line of defense from Kentucky to Alabama. Liberty was one of the main points on this line and was occupied by about 1000 Confederate cavalrymen under the command of Gen. John Hunt Morgan, whose headquarters was at McMinnville. A few other troops were stationed around Liberty and Alexandria, including R.D. Allison's cavalry squadron, made up mostly of DeKalb Countians.

Opposing the Confederate forces were various Union regiments, mostly under the command of Gen. John T. Wilder and

Col. William B. Stokes. These Union forces attacked both
Alexandria and Liberty on February 3, 1863, attacking Liberty
again on February 17. On both occasions the Confederates retreated to Snow's Hill. On March 17, however, when another at-
tack was made on Liberty, the Confederates pursued the Union
forces to Milton, where a battle was fought for some hours, with
the Confederates suffering about 300 casualties. On April 2, 1863,
the Union forces attacked again at Liberty, beginning the heaviest fighting in DeKalb County during the entire war. Morgan's
men retreated during the night to Snow's Hill, which they thought
they could hold. However, Col. Joseph Blackburn led the Federal troops up the Mann Hill Road to cut them off at the rear.
The Confederates escaped the trap, but only by a hasty and cha-
otic retreat in which they were "stampeded like cattle on the prai-
rie." Both sides ran out of ammunition, and the Federals returned
to Murfreesboro. The battle engaged about 2000 men on each
side. There were several casualties; some of the dead were buried near the Atwell schoolhouse, while the wounded were treated
at various houses along the road, including Dr. John A. Fuson's
on Dry Creek.

After this battle General Wilder's men burned the steam-operated gristmill and William Vick's store at Liberty and damaged
the steam mill at Alexandria. They marched up Smith Fork and
the Caney Fork, taking mules and horses wherever they went,
along with corn, hay, hams, chickens, and whatever else they could
find. As if this were not bad enough, Morgan's men and horses
returned to Liberty within two weeks of the battle and they, too,
had to be fed from the surrounding farms. Though they paid
for what they took, they still took. By the end of April 1863 much
of DeKalb County was in pitiful shape. Meat, corn, and wheat
were all gone, and no more could be grown; there were no mules
and horses with which to plow, and no men to do the plowing.
Mercifully, Morgan's men were soon gone; on June 11, 1863,
they gathered at Alexandria and left on their greatest raid, one
which carried them through Indiana and Ohio to the farthest
point north reached by any Confederate troops.

Both Confederate and Union sympathizers hoped that DeKalb

Still standing in Liberty is the childhood home of Will T. Hale, author of the first history of DeKalb County. During the Civil War Liberty was a center of military activity, much of it witnessed by Mr. Hale from this house.

County could live in relative peace once the opposing armies were gone from the county. This was not to be, however; the remaining two years of the war were to be the most difficult ones of all. By the middle of 1863 the county government in DeKalb had practically stopped. There were no courts, there were no schools, and very few church meetings were held between 1862 and the end of the war. When the armies left there was no authority, and gangs of guerrillas, known as bushwhackers, took over. Some were Federal sympathizers and some were Confederate sympathizers, so that the citizens of the county were victimized by one group if not by the other, and no one was safe.

The Mine Lick gang was active on the Caney Fork; most of its victims were Confederate sympathizers. On Falling Water, this gang not only killed Billy Robinson's geese and hogs, they took the family's clothes as well. Mrs. Ellen Bozarth's home was burned to the ground by bushwhackers, and her son-in-law, Dick Smith was killed by them. The taking of such items as horses, hams, and chickens was a commonplace offence by this group.

Indian Creek and Holmes' Creek had their own group of

bushwhackers, also generally of Union sympathy. They not only engaged in such activities as taking horses, but they also killed several people. Among their victims were Henry Hendrixson, Henry Turner, and Ezekiel Taylor, a 60-year-old former sheriff.

The most notorious of all the gangs of bushwhackers was the one led by Pomp Kersey, which was active mainly around Liberty and Smithville. Referred to by a Union officer as "regular desperadoes," they acquired a formidable reputation. The Liberty neighborhood dreaded their visits, especially after they shot and killed Ben Blades through the door of his own house. They were more welcome at Smithville, where Confederate sympathizers were happy to see them chase away a group of recruiters for the Union army. Later the bushwhackers became less discriminating about who they bothered; they took money from William G. Foster and John M. Love, both of whom had sons in the Confederate army. Several of this band of guerrillas had served in the Confederate army, including the leader Hiram T. (Pomp) Kersey. Pomp enlisted in Company A, 16th Tennessee Infantry Regiment, in 1861, when he was only thirteen years old. When the Confederate army left Middle Tennessee in the summer of 1863 Pomp left the army and returned to his home near Short Mountain. A band of Union bushwhackers had been active there, and Pomp hoped to protect his home against their outrages. Unfortunately, he and his band were soon doing similar things, and were much wanted by the Union army. After less than a year of guerrilla activity, they attacked a group of Union soldiers who were attending a party near Gassaway on the night of July 23, 1864. The next day the Union men tracked the Kersey band to their hiding place near Short Mountain. Finding the bushwackers asleep, the soldiers took them by surprise and killed all but two or three. Pomp Kersey almost escaped, but was shot by Bill Hathaway and Thomas G. Bratten. Bratten was a month older than Kersey; both were 16 years old. Brought to Liberty in an oxcart, the bodies were buried nearby. Pomp Kersey's body was later moved to the Melton Cemetery near Short Mountain and buried under a tombstone which reads, "He Died for His Country."

Besides the guerrilla bands, the regular armies of both sides were still passing through the county. Union troops under Stokes and Blackburn were stationed at Liberty and at Alexandria, where they camped on the fairgrounds. In the late summer of 1864 Capt. Jack Garrison's company of Union soldiers began building a stockade or fort at Liberty, but this was interrupted by the passage through the county of part of the Confederate army under the command of Gen. Joe Wheeler. The passing Confederate forces helped themselves to most of the few remaining horses in the county.

The Federal stockade at Liberty was completed later that year, but no more Confederate troops came into DeKalb County, so it was never used in a battle. Lee surrendered in Virginia in April of 1865 and Joe Johnston in North Carolina a short time later. The last of DeKalb County's Federal soldiers were discharged in August of 1865, and the Civil War in DeKalb County was ended.

DeKalb Countians in the Civil War

DeKalb County paid a high price in blood for its part in the Civil War: in no other war have so many DeKalb Countians been involved; in no other war have so many bled and died. Before the war was over more than 2000 DeKalb County men had served as either Confederate or Union soldiers, and a dozen or more had even served in both armies. None of the surrounding counties had as many Union soldiers as did DeKalb County; in fact, DeKalb had more Union soldiers than did all the six surrounding counties combined. Twelve Union companies and 14 Confederate companies were comprised mostly of DeKalb Countians. The Confederates served longer than the Federals; most of the Confederate companies were enlisted during the first year of the war, while most of the Federal companies did not enter service until the last year of the war. The DeKalb County Confederates fought in many terrible battles, traveled great distances, and suffered from hunger, cold, sickness, and death. Though DeKalb County's Federal soldiers had no easy time of it, they were furnished uniforms, shoes, and food. Few of them left Tennessee; few of them were in major battles, and few of them were killed or wounded.

The Confederates began enlisting in April of 1861, immediately after Fort Sumter and two months before Tennessee seceded from the Union. The system of enlistment was different from that of later wars. In the Civil War, men of a certain area would organize themselves into a company and elect a captain, then join with other companies to form a regiment. It was the ultimate in democracy; all officers were elected. In April of 1861 John F. Goodner, a Mexican War veteran, organized at Alexandria the group which became Company A, 7th Infantry Regiment. Robert Cantrell of Smithville organized Company E of the 23rd Infantry Regiment during the same month. In May, Companies A and G of the 16th Infantry were organized by P. C. Shields and L. N. Savage, whose brother John H. Savage, was elected colonel of the regiment. In August of 1861 Company F, 24th Infantry Regiment, was organized by R. D. Allison; the following month John Pack organized Company I, 35th Mountain Rifles Regiment. During the last month of 1861 two more companies of Confederate infantry were organized when Matthew T. Martin and Perry Adcock enlisted men in Company A and Company C of Colms' 1st Battalion. The last company of Confederate infantry was enlisted by S. B. Whaley almost a year later, in November of 1862; it became Company E of the 84th Regiment.

Since the Confederate army did not furnish horses, only a few from the county joined the Confederate cavalry, as most could not afford to take their own horses to war. However, there were a few DeKalb Countians in T. M. Allison's Company E of the 1st Cavalry Battalion, organized in June of 1861. Martin B. Foutch's Company F, 11th Cavalry Battalion, was organized the following December with some DeKalb County members. The three companies of R. D. Allison's cavalry squadron, which consisted mostly of DeKalb Countians, were organized in the fall and winter of 1862–1863.

DeKalb County's Confederate soldiers were involved in almost every major battle of the war. John F. Goodner's company was sent to Virginia in July of 1861 and remained there until Lee's surrender at Appomattox in 1865, although death, disease, imprisonment, and savage battles left only a few members of the company present at the surrender.

Robert Cantrell's company was also in Virginia at the end of the war, but most of the DeKalb County companies were in the Army of Tennessee. This did not mean that they spent all their time in Tennessee, by any means. Some idea of their travels is given from the records of M. T. Martin's and Perry Adcock's companies. They traveled first to Nashville, and then to Fort Donelson, where in February of 1862 the entire garrison surrendered and was sent to prison in Ohio and Indiana. At the end of the summer they were exchanged at Vicksburg, Mississippi. They then spent three months at Port Hudson, Louisiana, and in September of 1863 were ordered to Chattanooga. A train collision in Georgia killed Capt. M. T. Martin and several others; the companies also suffered heavy casualties in the battles of Chickamauga and Missionary Ridge. In February of 1864 they were sent by rail to Demopolis, Alabama. The threat there soon passed, however, and ten days later they were back at Dalton, Georgia, having traveled 872 miles. Martin's and Adcock's companies joined the fight against Sherman's army through the summer of 1864. Withdrawing from Atlanta in September, they returned as part of John B. Hood's army to Tennessee, where they were engaged in November in the Battle of Franklin, followed by the defeat of Hood's army at the Battle of Nashville. Their bare feet bleeding, they retreated over the frozen ground to Alabama. Their last journey was made by rail, to join Gen. Joseph E. Johnston's force in North Carolina, where no more than half a dozen members remained of the two companies when they surrendered in April of 1865.

Other DeKalb County Confederate companies traveled about as much as did Martin's and Adcock's companies. Savage's and Shields' companies served in Virginia, South Carolina, and Mississippi before fighting at the Battle of Perryville in Kentucky. After the Battle of Murfreesboro, they fought at Chattanooga, after which they followed the same route as Martin's and Adcock's companies.

The Confederates suffered enormous casualties, which began long before they ever went into battle. In the first training camp several died of measles; others died in camp of typhoid, malaria, pneumonia, and diarrhea. These last two were also common causes of death among those who were captured and sent to the Northern prisons. In fact, so many died in prison that some decided anything was better than remaining there. At Rock Island Prison in Illinois Leonard Cantrell, Levi Cantrell, and Daniel Cantrell joined the U. S. Army and went to Kansas to fight the Indians. All had been in Savage's company, as had John LaFever, who left the same prison to join the U.S. Navy.

In addition to death from disease and imprisonment, there were the battlefield casualties. The Civil War was fought in the old European style, with the men of one side lining up elbow to elbow charging against the men of the other side. By 1861 rifles were greatly improved and had become so deadly at long range that such charges should have been abandoned. They were not, however, and enormous casualties on both sides, especially among the infantry, resulted. John H. Savage's 16th Regiment suffered 200 casualties in the Battle of Perryville on October 8, 1862. Less than three months later they went into the Battle of Murfreesboro with 400 men; 205 of them were killed, wounded, or missing in that disastrous battle. Among the wounded was Capt. L. N. Savage of Company A; he suffered in agony for 72 days before he finally died. Company A of the 16th had 147 men at the beginning of the war; when the army surrendered four years later, only seven remained.

DeKalb County's Federal units did not suffer nearly as heavy casualties as did the Confederates. This was true partly because the Federals were in the cavalry, partly because they were in fewer major battles, and partly because they served less time. Most DeKalb County Confederates had already been in service for a year or more before the first DeKalb County Federals enlisted in Stokes' 5th Regiment in July of 1862. Two companies enlisted at that time; another enlisted the following February. Most of the DeKalb County Federals, however, did not enlist until September of 1864, when Joseph Blackburn organized his 4th Regiment of Tennessee Mounted Infantry. Blackburn had served

Confederate veterans at a reunion at Seven Springs about 1910. The occasion was not marred by the fact that the first owner of the resort had been a Union army captain, nor by the fact that some of these veterans had left the Confederate army without official leave. *In the first row are:* Fielding Turner, Joe Ray, Sice Green, Nathan Wall, J. M. Redmon, Dick Webb, Jim Stoner, Newt Avery, and Bill Tippett. *In the second row are:* Son Hicks, Wat Cantrell, Tom Jones, Jim Dawson, Pat Cantrell, John Loring, John Vanhooser, James Monroe Rankhorn, John Cotton, John Womack, W. B. Ward, Ed Hodge, and Cap Rose.

first in Stokes' Regiment, as had Jack Garrison, who organized Company G of the 1st Regiment of Tennessee Mounted Infantry.

Strangely enough, many of those who enlisted in the Union army were slaveowners or the sons of slaveowners. The areas around Liberty and Smith Fork had a large number of slaveholders, yet this is where most of DeKalb's Union soldiers lived. On the other hand, the area south of Smithville had very few slaveowners, but almost all the men from this area enlisted in the Confederate army. DeKalb Countians generally seemed to follow the pattern of the political parties before the war. Those who had been Democrats went with the Confederacy and remained Democrats after the war. Those who had been Whigs before the war remained loyal to the Union and became Republicans after the war. There were exceptions, of course, but this was the general pattern. DeKalb County had many more men in the Federal army than did any adjoining county, probably due largely to the influence of William B. Stokes.

Colonel Stokes seems to have been more successful at getting men into the Union army than at getting military discipline into them after they enlisted. In fact, discipline in the 5th Cavalry Regiment became so poor that in June of 1864 it was sent to Tullahoma under the command of General Milroy, while Colonel Stokes was placed in command of the Federal post at Carthage. Six months later, General Milroy reported that he had "tried every means known to me to bring about order and efficiency in the regiment, but have not been rewarded with any success. . . . The field officers seem to have no conception of their obligations and duties; have no control over their subordinates or men. Officers and men absent themselves without authority whenever they take a notion to visit their homes." He suggested that Colonel Stokes be put back in command of the regiment, but this was not done.

However, Colonel Stokes was in command during most of the military action in which the 5th Cavalry took part. They were in the Battle of Murfreesboro and in many of the skirmishes around Liberty in 1863. They suffered their heaviest casualties on February 22, 1864, when a scouting party under Capt. Ezekiel W.

Bass was ambushed in White County by Champ Ferguson's guerrillas. Ten men were killed and several wounded, with about forty casualties in all.

The capture of Champ Ferguson was the most notable accomplishment of Joseph Blackburn, who organized the 4th Mounted Infantry Regiment in September of 1864, after he resigned as captain of Company A of Stokes' Regiment. Only 22 years old when he was mustered in as lieutenant colonel of his regiment, the handsome Blackburn usually rode into battle with a plume in his hat. He did not battle Champ Ferguson; in fact, Ferguson claimed that he was captured by trickery and that Blackburn told him he would be treated like all Confederate soldiers. However, on October 20, 1865, five months after his capture, Ferguson was hanged, the only Confederate guerrilla to be so treated.

Colonel Blackburn's regiment was mustered out of service on August 25, 1865. Stokes' 5th Cavalry Regiment had been mustered out ten days earlier; there were no more DeKalb Countians in either army. The Civil War was over, though its effects would not be over for years to come.

After the War

The end of the Civil War found DeKalb County in dire circumstances. Many men would never return, many who did return had lost arms or legs. Mills had been destroyed, houses and barns had been burned, and much livestock had been killed or stolen. Worst of all was the division between the former Confederates and the former Union soldiers. They had fought on opposing sides during the war, and they were still on opposite political sides after the war. Practically all the Confederate veterans supported the Democratic party, while practically all the Union veterans became Republicans following the war.

During the first four years after the war, the Confederate veterans were not permitted to vote. The political contests were within the Republican party, which was divided into Conservative and Radical factions. William B. Stokes of DeKalb County, who had served as U.S. Representative prior to the war, was again elected to Congress, this time as a Radical Republican. Though prevented from taking office for several months until Tennessee ratified the Fourteenth Amendment, Stokes was an important leader among the Radical faction of Republicans. When Governor Brownlow was sick in 1867 Stokes campaigned throughout Tennessee on his behalf. Brownlow was reelected governor, and Stokes was asked to campaign in New York for the Republicans, and again conducted a successful speaking tour. Stokes was less successful in his campaigning in Tennessee in 1869 when he ran for governor against fellow Republican DeWitt C. Senter. Stokes lost by more than two to one, and even failed to carry DeKalb County in this election. In 1870 he also failed to be reelected to Congress. The Radical Republicans had lost their strength in Tennessee and in DeKalb County, as indeed had the Republican party in general.

By 1870 former Confederates were voting again, and Democrats were generally in control. In DeKalb County, however, some Republicans were elected to county offices in almost every election. There was great rivalry between the parties, and elections were hard fought. It was generally considered that the ends justified the means, and almost any means were used to win an election. Votes were bought, extra ballots were added to the boxes, and entire ballot boxes were stolen on their way to the county seat. Party affiliation was strong for many voters, and such loyalties were passed down from one generation to the next. For instance, in the Jefferson community more than one dying Confederate veteran gathered his children and grandchildren about his deathbed and with his last breath commanded them to promise never to vote for a Republican. With a backbone of such loyalty in both Democratic and Republican parties, almost every election in DeKalb County was a bitter contest.

Violence and racism were major legacies of the war, making the entire era to 1900 a turbulent one in the county. While the majority of DeKalb's citizens wanted to live in peace and forget the recent conflict, some just could not do so. Twenty years after the war fights and murders were still being caused by wartime grudges. Violence was particularly prevalent in the Caney Fork area, especially on Wolf Creek and Mine Lick. Several murders occurred in the county during this period, and the violence of the era culminated in a mob lynching at Smithville in 1901. The victim of this particular lynching was not black, although many DeKalb Countians would have been pleased to lynch a black man.

The freed slaves were given voting privileges in Tennessee in 1867, and the Union League was formed to encourage blacks to vote for Radical Republicans. The former Confederates, who could not vote at all, found this intolerable, and some of them organized the Ku Klux Klan to try to control the blacks to some extent. Still, there was perhaps less antagonism towards blacks in DeKalb County than in many parts of Tennessee. There were two cases of whippings of blacks in DeKalb County, and at least one Ku Klux Klan member was indicted. Ward Hickman, a black man, was murdered near Long Branch about 1890 by a so-called Ku Klux Klan group. Not all the Ku Klux Klan victims were black; in 1872 "night riders" burned the home of Wilson Taylor, a former Union soldier. He and his family moved to Illinois and never returned.

While blacks were unquestionably held in a position inferior to whites, they were able to make considerable advances. A few of them stayed on with their old owners, but by 1870 most had moved away. A number of former slaves were able to own a few acres of land, and there was very little of the sharecropping system that grew up in much of the South. Black men were employed chiefly as farm laborers, and the women, especially around the towns, were employed to do laundry and to cook. In fact, the reputation of black women as excellent cooks was such that often they could get jobs when whites could not.

Black churches and schools were also established early in DeKalb County. In 1867 the mayor of Alexandria deeded land by the cemetery for a black church and school. Yandle Wood wrote from Alexandria that "the Coloured school at this place meets with very little opposition, not as much as I expected." This was in contrast to nearby Carthage, where the black school was burned and the teachers warned to "go North where they belonged."

The three decades following the Civil War saw a gradual migration of DeKalb County's blacks into towns, where there was less racial prejudice than in some of the rural areas. Though the schools were completely separate, the churches were not, and the Smithville Church of Christ had at least one black member, Tennie Williams. There was never a segregated housing pattern; in all the towns blacks and whites lived side by side with no apparent conflict. In Liberty, as early as 1870, more than a third of the black residents were property owners. By 1900 Adam Crowder, a black barber of Smithville, lived in a substantial home on the turnpike between the courthouse and the present Joe L. Evins home.

Home Life, 1860–1914

Homes and home life did not change a great deal in the 50 years between the end of the Civil War and the beginning of World War I. Kerosene, or "coal oil" as it was called, had just become available in 1865, and it was still the main source for light in DeKalb County homes in 1914. Telephones were becoming common by 1914, and a few families owned automobiles, but horses and feet still provided most transportation. And during all those years, the home was where all births, sicknesses, and deaths took place, as well as most weddings and funerals. Almost all houses in DeKalb County during this half-century were built of wood. Some were very elaborately trimmed with Victorian gingerbread, but by no means all; a number of log houses were also built during this period.

The furnishings varied likewise. Several houses in the towns and on the more prosperous farms had parlors furnished with a velvet parlor suite, a carpet, and a marble-topped center table with an elaborate lamp and a family album. Other families spent their lives in a single room which contained two or three beds, a few chairs around the fireplace, a clock on the mantel, and little else. Prior to the Civil War, some houses had kitchens, while in others the women cooked at the only fireplace they had. After the war most families eventually built a room for use as a kitchen, mainly because of the increasing use of the cookstove. By 1890

The home of Tom Potter, a prosperous Smithville merchant, was on South College Street. Pictured here about 1895 on the porch are Mary McGuire, the housekeeper, and the Potter sons Kelly, John, and Thomas. Seated on the bench are Tom Potter and his wife, Samantha West; their daughter Elizabeth is at the easel. Another daughter Lillian is on the horse, flanked by Sam Whiteley, and his wife Betty, the cook. In the tree is a neighbor boy. Note that even the prosperous had no screens on their windows.

most families owned a cookstove and had abandoned the fireplace for cooking.

What they cooked varied widely. Mattie Blankenship Cheatham, daughter of a Smithville merchant, recalled that when she was growing up in the 1880s her family always had plenty of everything to eat. And when there was company to eat a meal Mattie's mother would serve fried chicken, fried ham, roast beef, green beans, lima beans, peas, Irish potatoes, sweet potatoes, okra, corn, cooked tomatoes, raw tomatoes, corn bread, biscuits, light bread, cake, fruit cobbler, egg pie, and molasses pie—all this at one meal—along with whatever else might be in season. By contrast, a boy who also grew up in the 1880s, the son of a tenant farmer on Eagle Creek, said that his mother had to sell most of the eggs they got in order to pay for salt, needles, and things they had to have from the store. For him, the finest meal he could even imagine was a fried egg and a hoecake.

Most clothing during this period was made at home, though about 1900 ready-to-wear clothes became available, first for men, and later for women. Prior to that time, clothing was made at home, either from "factory cloth" or from home-woven cloth. The spinning wheel and the loom were still in use for many years after the Civil War. Most farmers had a small cotton patch for home use, as well as a few sheep to provide wool. Yarn spun from this wool was used by mothers to knit stockings and socks for the entire family; this was common practice until well after 1900.

There were few closets in houses, and there was little need for them. In this day of cheap and plentiful clothing, it is almost impossible for us to imagine how few clothes DeKalb Countians owned a century ago. For example, many women owned a Sunday dress and one or two everyday dresses, and that was all. Of course, there were those who had more and dressed very fashionably. The women of Alexandria were noted for being very stylish dressers, but they had plenty of competition in Liberty, Smithville, and other areas of the county. Even these fashionable dresses were made at home; Judge B. M. Webb's wife made for her three daughters very elaborate dresses, with bustles, leg-o-mutton sleeves, and endless yards of lace, ruffles, and flounces, all in the latest style.

Some hats were made at home, but most were not, especially the more stylish ones. Hats were an essential part of everyone's dress—no man, woman, or child would think of going outside the house for any length of time without a hat of some sort.

One new article of clothing that appeared in DeKalb County just before World War I was the bathing suit, though there were actually very few of them. Most men and boys continued to enjoy their swimming as they always had, without benefit of any clothing at all. However, a few young ladies had now begun to venture to "the swimming hole." Dr. T. J. Potter's daughter Willie was one of these daring young women. Her bathing suit, however, was anything but daring. Made of green mohair, it covered her from wrist to ankle.

Swimming was probably the most strenuous form of recreation that DeKalb Countians indulged in. Most people were doing such strenuous work every day that they were glad to rest on their few days off. There were occasional play-parties and some square dances, though dances were condemned by many churches. Hunting and fishing were not really considered recreation at this time though family reunions, picnics, and long walks were. Other recreations were games of checkers, an occasional baseball game, and around 1900, the new game of croquet.

Croquet was about the most athletic activity engaged in by the guests at the Seven Springs resort hotel. Located on Sink Creek seven miles south of Smithville, the large hotel was opened in the 1890s by Beverly W. Robinson and his father W. T. Robinson of Dowelltown. The seven springs were of black sulphur, red sulphur, and so on, and were said to cure a number of diseases. For 25 years or more the resort attracted summer visitors from DeKalb County and from as far away as Nashville. Besides drinking the waters, the main activities of the guests seemed to be eating three excellent meals a day and rocking on the long porches. The Seven Springs Hotel became a sort of community center and for several years was host to a large Fourth of July celebration and to the reunion of DeKalb County Confederate veterans.

Economic Development

Transportation

DeKalb County's first settler arrived in 1797; in 1798 John and Leonard Fite with others cut the first road to Liberty and brought in the first wagon. The earliest roads were full of stumps and ruts, had little or no gravel on them, and were so narrow that two wagons could not pass. Rivers and creeks had to be forded, since there were no bridges. Jesse Allen established a ferry on the Caney Fork at the mouth of Eagle Creek as early as 1813.

Some idea of the condition of DeKalb County's roads can be gained from this 1905 view of Smithville's Main Street one block west of the courthouse. This was the best road in the county, being not only the main street of the county seat but also a part of the Lebanon-Sparta Turnpike.

He also built a road on either side of the river leading to the ferry, and by the 1820s there was regular stagecoach service on this route through Liberty and Alexandria to Nashville. While roads were cleared leading to Carthage, McMinnville, and Sparta, the main road was and is the one leading to Nashville, the urban and trading center for this area.

In December of 1837 a company was incorporated to build a new turnpike from Lebanon toward Sparta. Covered bridges were built at Liberty and at Dowelltown, and the road went up Snow's Hill, whereas the old road had previously gone up Dry Creek and out the Mann Hill Road. Another major change was that the crossing of the Caney Fork was moved from Allen's Ferry four miles upstream to Sligo, where a new ferry was established. The turnpike was privately owned, of course; four tollgates were established within the county, and a charge was made to travel on the road. Both the tollgates and the ferry were in use until after 1925.

Daniel Alexander's home at present-day Alexandria was used as a tavern as early as 1802; the Duncan Tavern in Liberty was built early enough to have Andrew Jackson as a guest. The building of the turnpike brought a demand for more taverns and hotels. The Browning Tavern and the Reese Tavern were operated at Alexandria before the Civil War. Luke McDowell and Thomas

Bradford kept inns at the top of Snow's Hill, as did Mrs. Rachel Beckwith, who operated the well-known Beckwith Inn where Andrew Jackson also stayed as a guest. In 1850 the Masonic Lodge built a two-story frame hotel of fifteen rooms which stood for almost a century where the City Hall now stands on the east side of the square in Smithville. Hotels remained in demand for many years; as late as 1940 Edgar Evins built a two-story twenty-room hotel in Smithville; it is now used as the Sha-Lee Apartments.

Sligo was not only the site of the ferry on the Caney Fork; it was also considered the head of navigation for steamboats on that river. The first steamboat on the Caney Fork was the *Harry Hill*, which was built on Smith Fork in 1832 by Samuel Caplinger and William Christian and then floated down to Nashville to have its machinery installed. Returning to Carthage the same year, it made its way to Sligo on high water. The Caney Fork was not navigable during low water, so winter and spring were generally the times when the steamboats made their trips up the river. Landings were established at Wolf Creek, Holmes' Creek, and other points, with Sligo the last landing, although a few steamboats came as far upriver as Shippingport, near the mouth of Sink Creek. Local residents came to these landings with hogs, corn, poultry, eggs, hides, furs, molasses, hams, etc., and shipped them down to Nashville by steamboat.

The 20 years before the Civil War marked the high point of steamboat traffic on the Caney Fork. Some residents of the area worked on steamboats: M. T. Martin was clerk at about $75 a month and David James was a navigator at about $100 a month; both were excellent wages for the time. A. L. Davis in 1846 was captain of a steamboat named the *Caney Fork*. A number of people traveled to Nashville by steamboat, and John Stagg Allen's daughter Elenora made the trip to New Orleans. Just before the Civil War young Dora Pistole, accompanied by her mother, not only made the trip to New Orleans (which took about 10 days), but sailed over the Gulf of Mexico, crossed the Isthmus of Panama, and traveled on to California, where they visited relatives of her deceased father before returning to DeKalb County.

Following the Civil War, Bird S. Rhea moved from his farm

near Sligo to Nashville, where he and his son Isaac T. Rhea were very active in the steamboat business and in grain trading. They kept steamboats coming up the Caney Fork; in 1887 eight steamboats were making regular trips up the river. One was named the *B. S. Rhea*, and over the years several were named *Caney Fork* and *Sligo*. Steamboat traffic gradually declined after 1900 and had practically ended by 1920, though small boats still traveled the river until World War II.

The Caney Fork served not only as a thoroughfare for steamboats, but as a means of getting commercial timber from the DeKalb County hills to the Nashville mills. This was done by fastening the logs together to form rafts, which were then floated down the river. The rafts were 30 to 40 feet wide and 80 or more feet long, with some sort of shelter for the crew of three or four men. The trip to Nashville took from six days to two weeks; like the steamboats, the rafts traveled only on high water. Rafting also declined after 1900, but a few rafts were run as late as the 1930s. Among those who ran rafts on the Caney Fork before 1910 were Dee Bozarth, Frank Cheatham, Ab Hooper, Tom Love, Charlie and Julius Ponder, George Puckett, Barn Taylor, C. D. Taylor, Riley Turner, and Jim and Pete Tittsworth.

Part of the reason for the decline of river traffic was the construction of the Tennessee Central Railroad about 1890. While the railroad did not enter DeKalb County, it did come close to the county's northern boundary at Brush Creek, Buffalo Valley, and Silver Point, and was of service to many DeKalb Countians. Efforts were made to bring a railroad into the county. In 1893 a charter was issued to the McMinnville and Smithville Electric Railway Company to build a railroad from McMinnville to Smithville and on to Silver Point, but the project never materialized. Nor did the proposed railroad from Smithville to Lebanon, for which a bond issue of $150,000 was authorized in a countywide referendum in 1916.

So DeKalb County remained primarily dependent on its roads for transportation. Public transportation was provided on the turnpike by the stagecoach until about World War I, when a motor "hack" ran from Smithville to the Watertown railroad depot.

In the 1920s Edgar Evins operated the Consolidated Bus Lines from Nashville to Smithville; the bus company ran profitably until sold to the Trailways system after World War II.

One of the main functions of the roads was to provide for carrying the mail. In earliest times residents had to go to Carthage, Sparta, or McMinnville to receive mail; but in 1808 a post office was established at Liberty, with Adam Dale as postmaster. By 1860 there were also post offices at Alexandria, Temperance Hall, Laurel Hill, Smithville, and Sligo. Thirty years later post offices had been established in almost every community in the county, with such names as Citadel, Truth, Joy, and Bear Branch. Most of these were eliminated by the rural free delivery system around 1900. A gradual consolidation of rural routes and post offices has reduced the present number of post offices in DeKalb County to four: Alexandria, Dowelltown, Liberty, and Smithville.

The early rural mail carriers were faced with plenty of problems, as few roads except the turnpike were passable in winter for any vehicle. In the hills and hollows the roads crossed and recrossed the creeks, and in many cases simply went down the creekbed. There were gates across the road in many places; one rural route out of Silver Point had seventeen gates across it. Roads in the flatwoods were different, but not necessarily better. In summer and fall they were inches deep in dust; in winter and spring they were seas of mud. When Richard Young covered his route on horseback in the winter, he sometimes arrived home with his boots frozen to the stirrups.

The coming of automobiles brought gradual improvement, but many roads were little better until after World War II. The first automobile in the county was bought by Edgar Evins in 1907, and soon there were many of them. In 1925 the turnpike was bought by the county and the toll gates eliminated. Bridges were built across the Caney Fork, as well as Smith Fork and other smaller streams. By 1929 many of the roads in the county were considerably improved. The Depression reduced funds for road improvement, however, as well as for buying automobiles. Many rural families were still using mule teams and wagons until after

World War II. Town residents often had neither automobile nor wagon, but walked everywhere they went.

The period of prosperity following World War II made cars and trucks available to nearly all DeKalb Countians. Almost all the roads were made at least passable, with most of them paved by the 1970s. In the early 1950s a major reconstruction was made of the old turnpike road; this is now U.S. Highway 70. It followed the general path of the turnpike, but eliminated many of the hills and curves. It also bypassed the old business districts of Alexandria, Liberty, Dowelltown, and Smithville; but crossed the Caney Fork on the new Sligo Bridge about where the old turnpike crossed. In the 1970s a similar reconstruction was made of Highway 56 from Smithville north to Interstate 40 at Silver Point.

Agriculture

For the first 150 years after its settlement, farming was the main business of DeKalb County. During that time the farm furnished most of what the family required. It certainly furnished all the food; it furnished the shelter; it furnished the fuel, and it furnished most of the clothing. Most farms had a few sheep and a cotton patch; carding, spinning, and weaving were family activities until 1900, and in some cases through the Depression of the 1930s.

Both crops and livestock were aimed primarily at feeding and clothing the family, so a considerable variety was grown on most farms. The leading crop by far was corn; in 1860 the average farm grew 500 to 1000 bushels of corn. In addition most farms produced 25 to 50 bushels of wheat and a few bushels of oats and rye. Each family raised 10 to 20 bushels of Irish potatoes and about twice as many sweet potatoes. Very little hay was grown until after 1900. Prior to that time livestock was largely wintered on fodder, which was pulled from corn while it was still slightly green and tied into binds. In some parts of the county, cattle could live on the cane which remained green all winter. In fact, tradition says that the main reason that the Dyer family moved to Mine Lick Creek in the 1830s was because of the plentiful supply of cane for their cattle.

Whippoorwill peas grew abundantly in the relatively infertile flat-woods land and provided a cash crop for the farmers. The Bud Knowles and Milligan Poss families are shown in the pea fields at Young Bend about 1915. The mules were named Callie and Kate.

Around 1930 burley tobacco became the chief money crop on most DeKalb County farms. It is still important on many farms, with the average farm growing around 2000 pounds. Tobacco was raised from earliest times in the county, though in those days it was dark-fired rather than burley. Tobacco production had almost died out by 1890, but in 1850 one farmer in five grew tobacco, averaging 2000 to 3000 pounds per farm.

One farm in five also produced honey, some in large amounts. Elisha Conger, Charles Ferrell, James Groom, Isaac Hill Hayes, and Ann Lee each produced more than 500 pounds of honey in 1850. Farms in the flatwoods produced very little honey, but after sorghum cane was introduced in the 1850s the flatwoods farms produced, on average, 25 gallons of molasses each. Some molasses was also made in the hill country. The gathering of neighbors at the molasses mill made a social occasion which was enjoyed by all, especially the children who played on the pomace pile (pomace being the cane from which the juice had been squeezed). Sorghum production has declined considerably since World War II, although a few families are still producing it for sale.

While horses were not the most plentiful livestock on the farm, they were by far the most valuable until they were replaced by tractors and trucks. An ordinary horse was worth ten to twenty times as much as a cow, and race horses such as those kept by Leonard Cantrell, Tan Fitts, and William B. Stokes were even more valuable. The raising of mules was an important business until they too were replaced by tractors after World War II.

Mules and horses had the best stables in the barn, as well as the best feed. Cows were lucky to stand in the hallway and get a few nubbins. Nevertheless, milk and butter were an important part of everyone's diet, and every farm had two or three cows for milk. Even in the towns, most families kept cows until milk became available in the stores in the late 1940s. Today most farm families buy milk at the store, and there are probably fewer than thirty families in the county who use milk from their own cows.

Beef cattle were in little demand for many years. Without refrigeration, beef did not keep; when a beef was killed, it had to be dried or sold or divided among several families. Consequently each farm had only two or three scrub cattle. When the national demand for beef increased in the 1940s a number of farmers developed large beef herds. Hereford and Black Angus were and are the most popular breeds, though some other breeds are grown today, such as Charolais and Santa Gertrudis.

Hogs were an entirely different matter. Hogs were brought in by the very first settlers and penned in the chimney corner to protect them from the wolves and wildcats. Soon, however, they were turned loose to roam, growing fat in the woods on acorns and beech mast; some of them turned wild. When James Bratten died in 1815 his inventory listed ten tame hogs and ten wild ones. By 1860 most farms had 25 to 30 hogs, and large families would kill 15 or 20 hogs in one winter. Salted and kept through the year, the pork served as the basic meat supply for the family.

From about 1840 to the Civil War, hog droving was a means of making money for several DeKalb Countians. Large numbers of hogs were driven to Georgia plantations where every acre was being planted to cotton; the plantation owners bought Tennessee hogs to feed their slaves and themselves.

Cotton production was attempted in DeKalb County in the

1920s, and a cotton gin was built at Smithville. The climate proved unsuitable, however, and cotton cultivation died out. Some cotton had been grown in the county in early times; 44 bales were produced in 1840. By 1850, however, the only cotton produced was in small patches for home use in spinning and weaving. Some flax was also grown for the same purpose, and most farms had a dozen or so sheep to furnish wool. Some flocks of sheep were kept until recent years in the hill country, but hardly any are now grown.

Before the Civil War the most valuable farms in the county were on Smith Fork. They were owned by Nicholas Smith at Temperance Hall, his brother Daniel Smith at Liberty, Edward Robinson below Dowelltown, William B. Stokes also below Dowelltown, his brother Thomas Stokes at Temperance Hall, and James Tubb at Hannah's Branch. Farms in that area of the county in 1860 were worth about $20 per acre. On the Caney Fork land was valued at $10 per acre, and in the flatwoods at only $5 per acre.

That ratio has changed considerably; in 1978 flatwoods land was bringing up to $4000 per acre, while Smith Fork land was bringing half that price, or less. The flatwoods land is more suitable for farming with tractors than is the hill land, and the soil in the flatwoods is suitable for growing nursery stock.

The growing of fruit trees for sale began around the 1880s in the area south of Smithville. John P. Tittsworth was one of the earliest nurserymen, followed by Jim Webb, F. P. Sanders, and others around 1900. Salesmen traveled to other states taking orders for shrubbery and fruit trees, and the nursery business has gradually expanded into a major source of income for the southern section of the county.

While nursery stock can produce a sizable income on a limited amount of land, it does require a great deal of hand labor. Some farmers have found that they can grow soybeans and corn as a money crop, using large and expensive machinery. This also requires a large number of acres, so that many who grow soybeans rent land.

There are presently about 1000 farms in DeKalb County averaging slightly more than 100 acres in size. Corn is still the leading crop, but the average amount raised per farm is about 250 bushels, only half what it was in 1860. Soybeans are also an important crop, but are raised mostly in the flatwoods area. Tobacco is the leading money crop and is grown all over DeKalb County. It presently brings about $1.75 per pound, but there is some doubt about the future of this crop because of its decreasing use, along with the importing of cheaper tobacco.

About half of DeKalb County's population is involved with farming in one way or another. Very few families now derive their total income from farming, however; almost everyone has some outside source of income.

Industry

Though farming was the main occupation for DeKalb Countians before the Civil War, a number of people were engaged in other jobs. There were blacksmiths, gunsmiths, hatters, shoemakers, saddlers, cabinetmakers, carpenters, and stonemasons. Several gristmills were in operation, along with sawmills, powder mills, cotton gins, tanyards, distilleries, crock kilns, and an iron furnace. The iron furnace was probably the most unusual industry to operate in DeKalb County. It was on Pine Creek just above the falls, and was established before 1817 by Jesse Allen and Elijah Gorman, who sold it in 1819 to Thomas Durham, Jr. In 1820 it employed 14 men and produced 30,000 pounds of bar iron each year. These 14 employees almost certainly did not include the makers of charcoal, for charcoal-making was almost an industry in itself. Besides iron ore and limestone, iron production required large amounts of charcoal for fuel. This in turn required enormous amounts of cut wood, and for that reason much land around Pine Creek was cleared long before it was used for agriculture. The crude iron produced by the furnace had to have further refinement, again using charcoal as fuel, before it became merchantable bar iron which could be used by blacksmiths to make tools, nails, horse shoes, etc. The iron furnace on Pine Creek ceased operations after about 25 years, when the supply of high-grade iron ore was exhausted.

Cripps' Mill on Dry Creek as it appeared about 1910. The group of visitors is unidentified, but the miller, Daniel Moser, is standing above the wheel while his son-in-law William Lee Edge is seated nearby. The first mill was established at this site in 1813.

Gristmills were probably the most common industry in DeKalb County, as well as the earliest. There was never a really satisfactory way to grind corn into meal or wheat into flour without the machinery of a mill. Adam Dale, the first settler, had a gristmill operating at Liberty by 1806, and within 20 years mills were established in most parts of the county. All the early mills were powered by water, though there were steam roller mills at Alexandria and Liberty by 1860. The steam-operated metal rollers crushed the grain more rapidly and were more efficient at separating bran from flour than the stones of a water-powered mill. Both of these steam mills were very profitable, as was the mill at Temperance Hall. Of the many gristmills which existed in DeKalb County, only a few remain. The one in most recent use is on Fall Creek about two miles east of Smithville. Established by James Lockhart before 1824, it was known as Webb's Mill from 1882 until 1937, when it was bought by Edgar Evins. Mr. Evins built a new mill and installed new machinery, but the mill was in operation for only five or six years. It was restored to working condition about 1980, but is no longer in operation.

Sawmills were often operated in conjunction with gristmills, and a sawmill was in operation at Liberty as early as 1812. Excellent timber was available over much of the county, and the demand for lumber was good since practically every structure in the county was made of wood. Four or five sawmills are still in operation, but most of the present home construction uses precut western lumber.

Distilleries were considered a necessary industry, as whiskey was an indispensable part of every household. Leonard Fite was operating a distillery in 1798, the year he moved to Smith Fork. By 1840 there were 13 distilleries in DeKalb County, producing an average of more than 1000 gallons each annually. Whiskey cost 40 cents a gallon, and the average family bought about a gallon a month, with more bought around Christmas. When the churches began to condemn all use of whiskey in the 1840s running a distillery became less respectable. However, distilleries continued to be operated in DeKalb County until Tennessee enforced prohibition in 1909. Prohibition increased the number of stills in the county, especially in the sections where the soil was very poor. If only a small crop of corn could be grown, it made sense to get the most profit from it. The making of illegal whiskey began to decline in the 1950s, and by 1980 very little was being made in DeKalb County. People still tried to circumvent laws pertaining to controlled substances, however, and several illegal patches of marijuana were destroyed in the county during the 1970s and 1980s.

The operation of a distillery required a good water supply, as did the operation of a tanyard. Matthias and William Anderson established a tanyard at Liberty by 1808, and the Goodner family operated a tanyard at Alexandria for many years before the Civil War. These tanyards were located near the creek, as was the one on the north side of Smithville. Owned in 1860 by W. J. Isbell, it was later bought by W. C. Potter and remained in operation until after 1900. There was also a tanyard three blocks south of the courthouse in Smithville, where Highway 70 now is. With tanyards on two sides of town, both Liberty and Smithville residents found it hard to escape their characteristic powerful smell. The tanyard, however, was a necessity for many years, for there was no rubber or plastic, and leather was used not only for shoes and boots, but for leather breeches and aprons as well as for harness and saddles.

Anyone who slaughtered a beef animal or had a cow die brought the hide to the tanner and either sold it to him or let him tan it for half the hide. As much as two years might pass before he got his half of the hide transformed into leather, for the tanning process was very slow. However, it yielded a better grade of leather than does the speeded-up modern tanning.

The employees of DeKalb County's tanyards were generally very strong men, for much of the work required great strength. Hides were soaked for several days, then scraped on both sides to remove hair, fat, and tissue. Tannic acid was what slowly changed a hide into leather; it came from black oak bark crushed into the size of a grain of wheat. The cleaned hide was soaked for several months in a weak solution of bark; then the hides were placed in a vat six feet long, four feet deep, and four feet wide. The alternating layers of bark and hides soaked here for as much as a year, during which they were occasionally turned. The hides were then washed, dried, and beaten before being sold to the local shoemakers and saddlers. The availability of shoes in stores and the coming of the automobile brought an end to the local demand for large amounts of leather.

Another industry which has now died out was the making of crockware. Beginning in the 1820s, this business lasted more than 110 years. The manufacture of churns, pitchers, grease lamps, and other articles of salt-glazed stoneware was carried on primarily by members of the LeFevre family and their relatives the Dunns, Elrods, and Hedgecoughs. The industry was centered around the Falling Water area where DeKalb County joins White and Putnam Counties. These three counties had by far the most extensive pottery manufacturing of any area in Tennessee. In what was essentially a family operation, clay was dug locally, turned into the desired shapes by hand, and fired in brick kilns. The pottery was peddled all over Middle Tennessee as well as being sold locally. Most pieces cost less than 25 cents each. There was a kiln by 1831 in the Narrows of the Caney Fork, owned by James Davis. Thomas Leek was the owner by 1840, though probably the LeFevres actually made the ware. By this time there were six crock kilns employing 15 men in the county. All of these were apparently in the Falling Water area of the Caney Fork. Newton Dunn operated a kiln at Bright Hill in the 1890s. The last kiln to operate in the county was the one located on the south side of Smithville. Its 35-year operation ended in 1915 with the death of the owner, John Washington Dunn.

Until after World War II there were no industries in DeKalb County which employed as many as 50 people. A small cotton factory in Alexandria in the 1840s used horse power and employed about 20 people. Around 1900 at Liberty a small factory made pins used on telephone poles; at Smithville there was a small spoke factory. In the 1920s a handle factory at Smithville employed about 20 people. About 1944 Layne Griffin began operation of a hosiery mill in Smithville. Though it lasted less than ten years, it was the beginning of the considerable industrialization which has continued to the present time. Garment factories have been the principal industry in DeKalb County; there are now two such factories at Smithville, and one each at Dowelltown, Liberty, Alexandria, and Peeled Chestnut. These garment factories employ about 1000 people, 900 of whom are women. Kingston-Timer, Nuturn, Texas Boot, and Hartmann Luggage are the only other large industries in the county, and they also employ more women than men. Many DeKalb County men have found factory work at Carrier in Warren County, at Ross Gear in Lebanon, and even as far away as Avco in Nashville.

Since about 1946 city and county officials, civic clubs, and businessmen have made almost continual efforts to bring industry to DeKalb County. The shirt factory in Smithville, begun in 1948, was the first major industry in the county. Edgar Evins was mayor of the town and had a large part in developing interest in industry. The DeKalb County Quarterly Court, with Judge Will Atwell presiding, agreed to construct the building for the shirt factory and lease it to Spartan Manufacturing Company. (The building is still county property.) The company needed $20,000 worth of equipment, so members of the Lions Club and some other businessmen agreed for 100 persons each to lend $200 to the company. This was paid back to the individuals at the rate of $20 each per year for ten years, with no interest.

Later industries were secured with similar efforts from civic leaders. In more recent years, grants from the Federal government have made possible the purchase of industrial land, while the issuing of tax-free industrial revenue bonds has made possible construction of industrial buildings. Industry in DeKalb County now provides jobs for about one third of the total work force, including a large number of women who rarely worked outside the home before World War II.

Business

For its first hundred years, DeKalb County's business community consisted mostly of general stores. Even in the towns there was hardly such a thing as a specialized store before 1900. F. Z. Webb's drugstore, the oldest continuously operated business in the county, was begun in Smithville in 1881. At that time it carried not only drugs but also a stock of shoes, and Mr. Webb met his wife, Amanda Smith, when she came in to look for a pair. Webb's drugstore in the 1930s sold house paint and school textbooks, and it still carries a surprising variety of merchandise today.

Even in the earliest times, the settlers could find quite a variety of goods at the stores. As early as 1806 they could buy velvet, red plush, and patent stockings, although most DeKalb Countians could not afford such finery. By 1810 Edward Foster of Carthage was keeping a store part-time at Liberty, where he sold goods for either cash or saltpeter. The first merchant to live in Liberty was Anthony Walke, who built both his store and his residence on the lot occupied in recent years by the home of Mr. and Mrs. Grover Evans. Mr. Walke was established before 1817 and doubtless had a stock of goods similar to the stores in Car-

DeKalb County's oldest business is F. Z. Webb and Sons Drug Store in Smithville, shown here as it appeared about 1919. *Left to right are* Caesar Webb, Sam Colvert, Athol Foster, Billy Christian, Ellis Dean, Zollie Webb (who began the store in 1881), Norval Webb, Jim Moore, and another customer.

thage, where silk and satin, ribbons and laces, coffee, loaf sugar, glassware, spices, and medicines were available. These could be traded for beeswax, tallow, rags, tobacco, hemp, or whiskey.

Gradually more stores were established in the towns. Joshua and James Bratten and Eli and William Vick were merchants in Liberty in 1850. Early Alexandria merchants were Joshua M. Coffee, James Goodner, Jacob Fite, and William Floyd. The Goodner family operated one of the best-known stores in the county; it endured for more than a century and was finally sold after World War II. Another Alexandria store which survived for many years was the D. W. Dinges Hardware Company, which began in 1865 and remained in the same family until the 1970s.

The years after the Civil War were apparently prosperous ones for the merchants of the county. In Smithville, William H. Magness was one of the earliest merchants, and probably the wealthiest. After the Civil War, his nephews W. C. Potter and T. B. Potter established stores in Smithville, as did his brother-in-law, R. B. West. All of these stores prospered, and the families later became involved in other enterprises. The Magnesses moved to McMinnville where they gave money for a library and other charities, while some of the Potters moved to Nashville and established what became the Commerce Union Bank. Mr. West was also involved in banking.

The earliest businesses were in Liberty, Alexandria, and Smithville, and most businesses remained in those towns until the Civil War. During the war commerce practically came to a halt, but the number of stores in DeKalb County gradually increased after the war. A few years before the Civil War, stores had been established at Temperance Hall and Wolf Creek, two of the county's more prosperous communities. This trend continued and by 1900 almost every community had its own general store, many of which also contained a post office. Though the post offices died out when rural routes were established, the stores generally remained in business. Several are still in business today, though there has been a gradual decline in the number since World War II.

Most of these country stores were general stores, but in the towns more specialized stores were established, especially after 1900. In Alexandria, Goodner's store and Lester's Department Store were noted places to buy ready-to-wear clothing, as was Conger Brothers in Smithville. This business occupied a handsome two-story brick building on the north side of the square, where they held spring and fall fashion shows until the store was destroyed by fire in 1931.

One of the Conger brothers, Alvin, was involved in the pearl business, as was his father, John Conger, and his brother-in-law, Jim Christian. The trading of freshwater pearls began around 1886 and continued until about the time of World War I. The mussels which abounded in the Caney Fork River produced pearls of excellent quality, though they were not easy to find. Usually hundreds of mussels had to be opened before one containing a pearl was found. Nevertheless, many were harvested from the Caney Fork, and Smithville was for some years a leading freshwater pearl market, with some pearls bringing well over $1000 each. In addition to the Congers and Jim Christian, Lon Crowley, S. L. Fitts, Brown Foster, John Smith, and John Windham all traded in pearls.

As the businessmen of DeKalb County acquired more money, there arose a need for banks. The first one in the county was established in 1888 in Alexandria, and was known as the Bank of Alexandria. In 1900 the Dinges Bank was established in Alexandria. Like Alexandria, Liberty had two banks: the Bank of Liberty, established in 1898 by A. E. Potter and his father-in-law, J. J. Smith; and the American Savings Bank, which opened in 1905. Smithville also had two banks. Potter's Bank, founded in 1892, was consolidated in 1901 with the Farmers and Traders Bank. The People's Bank and Trust was organized in 1903. With the lone exception of the Bank of Liberty, all these banks failed in the 1920s, and many citizens lost their savings. After these failures, new banks were established: Alexandria Bank and Trust Co., Dowelltown Bank, and First National Bank at Smithville. Eventually all four banks in the county came under the control of J. Edgar Evins. At his death in 1954, his son Joe assumed controlling interest of First National Bank, which later became First Central Bank under the control of James Ed Rice, a great-nephew of Edgar Evins. After being sold to a group of Nashville investors, First Central was one of 13 banks which failed in the Tennessee banking crisis of 1983. The bank was then purchased by City Bank and Trust of McMinnville and is in operation on the south side of the square in Smithville.

After Edgar Evins' death, the banks at Liberty, Dowelltown, and Alexandria came under the controlling interest of Mr. Evins' grandson, E. W. Evins. He eventually sold the bank at Liberty, built a bank at Smithville in 1974, and joined the three banks under the name of DeKalb County Bank.

Citizens Bank of Smithville was organized by a group of local investors in 1965. It has grown steadily since then, especially in the early 1980s, when it expanded both staff and building. Citizens Bank, City Bank and Trust, and DeKalb County Bank are the present banks of Smithville; DeKalb County Bank also has branches at Dowelltown and Alexandria, while Bank of Liberty has a branch at Alexandria as well as its main office in Liberty.

New business developments were brought about after 1910 by the increasing popularity of the automobile. Gasoline was necessary and for many years was dispensed from hand-operated pumps in front of general stores, as electric pumps were not used until the 1930s. Most service stations were rather makeshift affairs until after World War II, when their design became more functional. By the end of the war the last of the blacksmiths catering to the public had closed up shop and had been replaced by auto body and repair shops.

As horse-trading gradually died out, automobile dealing developed. There have been several short-lived dealerships in the county, but for many years there have been only two authorized ones, Amonett-Nixon (now Stribling) Chevrolet Co. and Smithville Motors (the Ford agency operated by John and Robert Alexander). Both agencies are in Smithville. There are also several used-car dealers in the county, including one at Liberty and one at Alexandria.

Increasing use of the automobile eventually brought a decline in the use of hotels, and today there is not a hotel in the county, though there are several motels in Smithville and around Center Hill Lake. As early as the 1920s restaurants were taking over one of the hotels' main functions by serving meals. Today there are in Smithville nine eating establishments, about half of which are fast-food places serving the automobile trade. There are also restaurants at Liberty and Alexandria and near Center Hill Lake. The number of business establishments in DeKalb County has increased greatly with the passing years, as has the number of people employed in them.

Social and Cultural Trends

The Healing Arts

It is no accident that "How are you?" is a standard greeting, for only a few years ago, most people had some sort of ailment. Often even the best-trained doctors could do little for them, and people suffered for years with conditions that could be easily corrected today. Death came early to many people: women died

Dr. Byron Parker owned one of the first automobiles in the county. Pictured here with him about 1912 are his wife, Novella West Parker, and in the back seat her father, Bob West, with his wife and their pet dog. The Parker home is in the background; it stood in Smithville on College Street just north of the Cumberland Presbyterian Church.

in childbirth, children died in infancy, and entire families died of malaria, tuberculosis, and typhoid fever, diseases which are hardly known today.

Doctors had little formal training; most of the early ones read a few medical books and served apprenticeships with established physicians before setting up their own practices. There were no examinations to pass; the State of Tennessee did not require physicians to be licensed until 1889. Most doctors learned how to deliver babies, how to set bones, and collected recipes to treat diseases. Tilman Bethel, born in 1788, was one of Liberty's first doctors. His recipe book included a cure for cancer, as well as a rheumatism ointment which called for toadfrogs and redworms to be boiled together with red pepper. Dr. Bethel apparently treated horses as well as humans, as his recipe book also contained a cure for the bots (an ailment affecting a horse's stomach).

Most people had to make do without the services of a doctor except for the most serious problems. Few people went to see the doctor; if they were sick enough to need him, they were too sick to go to him. So the doctors traveled long distances to see their patients, and often got little in return. The account book of Dr. John A. Evins showed that he was paid only 50¢ for a 20-mile house call. House calls were made regularly until well after World War II. Though Dr. J. L. Vanhooser had established a small clinic at Smithville in 1939, he made regular calls into Belk, Keltonburg, and other parts of the county during the 1940s, sometimes in a jeep driven by his friend Mrs. Bill Hill Young.

Few house calls were made in the years of early settlement, for there were few doctors. As late as 1840, there were seven doctors in the county, and six of them were at Liberty and Alexandria. In contrast, in 1980 there were seven doctors in the county, six of them located in Smithville. However, ease of transportation made those seven much more accessible than were the seven in 1840.

The doctors tended to locate in the towns. In 1860 there were four physicians in Alexandria, four in Smithville, and two in Liberty. However, they were beginning to settle in other locations; there was also a physician at Temperance Hall, one at Snow's Hill, and one on Dry Creek. By 1900 there were also doctors at Dowelltown, Wolf Creek, Mine Lick, Jefferson, Indian Creek, and Falling Water.

One of the earliest licensed physicians was Dr. Thomas J. Potter, who located in Smithville in 1893. He loved his work, and he was much loved by the families he served, as were many of the other doctors throughout the county. Perhaps this helped in some measure to repay them for long hours spent in travel and at bedsides, for before 1950, none of DeKalb County's doctors had more than a moderate income. DeKalb was a poor county, and many people had very little money. Dr. E. W. Dyer of Mine Lick had to operate a farm, for being a doctor in 1900 "had very little money in it" according to his wife, who became a mail carrier to supplement their income. Several of the other doctors also owned farms, including John A. Fuson of Dry Creek and R. M. Mason and S. C. Robinson, both of Temperance Hall.

DeKalb County physicians of the 1920s and 1930s included

Not only did several of the doctors own farms, but their wives were actively involved in operating them. Here in 1920 Mrs. Hatton Mason of Temperance Hall prepares to milk the cow. Mrs. Mason was the wife of Dr. Bob Mason, the mother of Dr. John Mason, the grandmother of Dr. Odell Mason, and the sister of Dr. Matt Wilson.

L. D. Allen, G. M. Allison, and C. A. Loring at Smithville; L. D. Cotten and J. R. Hudson at Alexandria; and W. H. Adamson and T. J. Bratten at Liberty. There is now no physician at Liberty or at Dowelltown. In 1977 Dr. David Darrah established his practice at Alexandria, following the death of Dr. Odell Mason in 1974. The present physicians of Smithville are Melvin Blevins, Hugh Don Cripps, W. W. Knowles, Jr., David Ours, Jerry Puckett, Jules A. Trudel, Kenneth Twilla, and J. C. Wall, Jr.

While DeKalb County now has excellent hospital facilities and surgery is a relatively routine matter, it was not always so. Through the 1950s and 1960s most surgery was performed at hospitals in Woodbury, Lebanon, or Nashville. In the 1920s and 1930s appendectomies and other emergency surgery were performed by Dr. C. S. McMurray of Nashville, who drove to DeKalb County and performed surgery in the patient's home, usually on the kitchen table.

All babies were born at home until 1939, when Dr. J. L. Van-

hooser established a small clinic in Smithville. This was expanded in 1948, and served as the principal medical center for
the county for many years. The county is presently served by
Doctors Hospital with 15 beds, built as Knowles Hospital in 1963,
and DeKalb General Hospital with 60 beds, built in 1970 by Hospital Corporation of America.

Dentists in DeKalb County have been somewhat scarcer than
physicians, and still are. Though there were traveling dentists in
the area by the 1850s, there was not a resident dentist in Smithville until Dr. J. T. Bell of Beech Grove set up his office in 1900.
Dr. Elisha Conger practiced a few years in Smithville before moving to Rockwood. Dr. R. L. Twilla took over Dr. Bell's practice
when Dr. Bell died in 1930. Dr. J. T. Duggin lived in Dowelltown,
but traveled to several other communities. Dr. Benedict and Dr.
Cotton were early dentists in Alexandria, but there had been no
dentist in Alexandria in recent years until Wesley Suddarth established a practice there in 1979. Other dentists of DeKalb County
at present are Larry J. Puckett and Jerry R. Hale, with his as-
sociate Cliff Duke, all of whom are located at Smithville.

Shortly after World War II, a chiropractor's office was established by Norman R. Atnip in his native Smithville, where he still
has a successful practice. He was joined about 1970 by his son,
Robert Roy Atnip.

Education

During the years of early settlement in DeKalb County, schools
were quite scarce and expensive as well. There were no public
schools; all were "subscription schools," where the teacher was
paid by the parents of the students who attended. The first school
in the county was very probably at Liberty, where there was a
school building in 1809. When the town of Alexandria was laid
out in 1820 a lot was donated for a school. In 1818 there was a
school on the ridge between Indian Creek and Holmes' Creek,
and gradually schools were built in other sections of the county.
As late as 1840, however, there were only ten schools in the county,
of which five were public and five were private. There was little
money for the public schools, and in 1850 the 34 public school

teachers received salaries of $16 per month for two months, which was as long as the school term lasted. Sometimes the teacher would stay on another month or two with those who could afford to pay. There was an average of nearly sixty pupils for each teacher. While the school term was short, the school day was long, and often lasted from sunrise to sunset. However, there was a morning recess, an afternoon recess, and an hour's break at noon, during which time the children jumped rope, played marbles, or chased each other over the hills in games of fox and hounds.

Most of the early school buildings were log with only wooden shutters for windows and split log slabs for benches. Such were the schools at Young Bend, Clear Fork, and Indian Creek. At Laurel School near Sligo in 1910, George Cantrell's hogs slept under the school and their fleas crawled through the floor and infested the pupils. Equipment was very limited; as late as the 1930s the total equipment issued to a teacher for the school year consisted of a water bucket and well rope, a broom, a box of chalk, and two erasers. The teacher also served as janitor.

The great majority of DeKalb County's citizens did not get an education beyond elementary school. This remained true until the late 1940s, when a countywide system of school buses was organized, funded from the state sales tax. Before that time it was hard for those who lived outside the towns to attend school beyond the eighth grade. Most simply could not afford it; those who could had to board away from home. Beginning in the 1920s high school students boarded in the towns with friends or relatives, or boarded at such schools as Baxter Seminary in Putnam County or Pleasant Hill Academy in Cumberland County.

Before the Civil War a few families were able to send their children away from home to attend schools at such places as Statesville, Gordonsville, Spencer, Murfreesboro, and Columbia. About 1850 Mr. William Ghormley opened a boarding school attended by about 40 young men and 20 grown girls. Located first at the mouth of Falling Water, the school was later moved near Smithville before closing by the time of the Civil War.

In addition to Mr. Ghormley's school, there were the Fulton Academy at Smithville and the Liberty Academy at Liberty; both were established in the 1840s. Shortly before the Civil War a Female Academy was established in Smithville and another at Alexandria. The Female Academy at Smithville apparently closed during the Civil War, but the one at Alexandria was still in use in 1886. The Turner M. Lawrence College, also at Alexandria, was established in 1858 and used until the 1930s. This school in the 1890s had about 100 pupils, ranging from the primary grades through junior college level. The subjects taught covered the same range, and included trigonometry, analytic geometry, physics, geology, French, Latin, and Greek. Both male and female pupils were taught, and some critics complained that there was "too much courting." The upper floor of the building was used by the Masonic Lodge; the lower floor was divided into three classrooms separated by canvas curtains. These could be rolled to the ceiling, creating a large auditorium with a stage at one end. The close of school brought "exhibition week," during which the music teachers presented their pupils in recital, the boys gave declamations, and the girls recited poems. Year after year the audience heard the impassioned plea that "curfew must not ring tonight" or grieved over the fate of wild Zangarella, the gypsy girl "whose lover had flown." So popular was the latter poem that one who recited it was followed twenty years later by her daughter reciting the same poem from the same stage. The members of the graduating class (probably no more than four or five) were more dignified; they usually read essays they had written for the occasion.

The Liberty Masonic Academy in the 1890s also had about 100 pupils; they paid tuition charges of $1.00 to $2.75 per month, depending on their grade level. Several of these pupils boarded at homes in Liberty; in the spring term of 1897 at least 16 young men were boarding there.

The Masonic Lodge took an active part in secondary education in DeKalb County and aided the schools at both Liberty and Alexandria. The school buildings at both places had a room reserved for the meetings of the Lodge; this remained so at Liberty until after consolidation of the high schools in 1963.

The Civil War had a drastic effect on education; practically all schools were suspended during the period. Most were slow to begin again and some never did. Many young people who should have been in school had to stay at home to work in the place of their fathers or brothers who had died or been crippled in the war. More than twice as many pupils were attending school in 1850 than in 1870, and the number of illiterate people increased greatly after the war.

Some recovery was made by the 1880s, and in that decade existed two of the best and best-known schools ever to operate in DeKalb County. One of these was at Smithville, where in September of 1883 a handsome new three-story brick building was opened for the use of the Pure Fountain College. It was so named by W. G. Crowley, one of the trustees, who expected it to be a "pure fountain of knowledge." Its college course offered Latin, trigonometry, astronomy, geology, bookkeeping, debate, vocal music, and calisthenics, and cost $5 per month per pupil. Tom Potter was president of the board of trustees; P. W. Dodson and T. B. Kelly were the college teachers. Equivalent to present-day high school and junior college, the school also included the primary grades, and in its first year had over 200 pupils

At about the same time in Alexandria the Masonic Normal School was being operated by H. L. W. Gross and James Boone, coprincipals. Mr. Boone taught all branches of mathematics and science, while Mr. Gross taught English, history, and foreign languages, including Latin, French, Greek, German, and Spanish. Music was taught by Mr. Boone's wife, Mattie, a graduate of the Cincinnati College of Music. The primary grades were taught by Mrs. Boone's sister, Miss Lunnie Wood. Many of the pupils at the Masonic Normal School were of college age; some came from as far away as Texas.

But regardless of the higher academic subjects that were taught in DeKalb County's colleges and academies, it was the one- and two-teacher schools that supplied the basic education for most DeKalb Countians. For many of them, it was their only education. These one-teacher schools were much alike all over the county: a log or frame building, simple wood benches or desks, a chalkboard if they were lucky. Practically every community had a school; in 1904 there were 80 one-and two-teacher schools in the county, some of them only two or three miles apart. In the days before electricity and easy transportation, these schools were a most important part of each community. The buildings served as churches, social centers, cultural centers, and voting places. Revivals and funerals were held in them, as well as candy drawings and pie suppers. These last two were fund-raising activities for the benefit of the school; the pie supper was especially popular in the 1930s and 1940s. The young ladies of the community were asked to make a pie and place it in a decorated box. These pies were then auctioned off; the highest bidder got not only the pie, but the privilege of eating it with the maker. Naturally there were those people in the community who enjoyed making someone pay a high price for the pie belonging to a special girl. If several in the audience had had a few drinks of whiskey they usually spent more freely, and sometimes one pie would bring $20 or more, an enormous price for that time. Among the other activities at the pie supper were cake-walks and the pretty girl contest, which was another big money-maker, as it also brought out competition in the audience. Money from the pie suppers was used for various projects, from buying pots and pans for the lunch room to buying uniforms for the basketball team. The people who lived nearby almost always gave strong support to the school in their community.

The name of one of the most obscure and isolated of these little one-room schools has been used over and over in recent years by businesses and civic organizations. This was Center Hill School, which was the one in the reservoir area nearest to the dam, and thus gave its name to Center Hill Dam and Reservoir, and to many other things. The Center Hill School was in many ways typical of DeKalb County's one-teacher schools. It originated in 1884 when W. E. Bartlett gave land for a church "to be a free House for all Christian people to preach in and hold meeting in." The Baptists were given priority for one week every summer or fall to hold protracted meeting. A log building was erected, and soon it came to be used as a school, taking the name Center Hill. Children living for several miles around walked there to school. Attendance varied but there were sometimes as many as 50 or 60 pupils for the one teacher. About 1910 a new frame building was erected; it too remained a center for community activities. There was a community Christmas tree in the school every year (people then had no Christmas trees in their homes), and there were plays for the public. Once, when Fantley Trapp was teaching there, young Riley Burton and his sister Sadie were featured in a play. Riley was supposed to say the blessing at a meal in the play, and Fantley left it up to him to use his own blessing. This proved to be a mistake, for when the play cast bowed their heads for the blessing, Riley said, "Durn the meat and damn the skin, open your mouth and cram it in!"

Several of the elementary schools in the county had basketball teams in the 1920s. They played on outdoor courts, of course, and most had both girls' and boys' teams. There was great rivalry among the various schools, and some of the better players repeated the eighth grade three or four times just to play basketball. From the 1920s through the 1950s a countywide tournament was held among these elementary school teams; the most frequent winners were the teams from Belk coached by Ollie Denton and teams from Walker's Chapel and New View coached by Floice Vickers. The high schools also had basketball teams, and the high school at Smithville had a football team beginning in 1926. The most successful football seasons were in 1938 when T. B. Webb was coach, in 1956 when Jim Lane was coach, and in 1979 when Wayne Cantrell and Mike DeRossett were coaches. High School basketball was generally more successful than football; in 1958 the DeKalb County High School boys' basketball team was one of 16 teams to participate in the state tournament. In 1959 the DeKalb County High School girls' basketball team won second place in the state tournament. Both of these teams were coached by Everett Lee Mitchell. Harold Luna was coach in 1965 when the girls' basketball team took fourth place in the state tournament.

Black athletes have played a part in DeKalb County's sports, but have not dominated as they have in some places. Schools for blacks and whites were separate until 1963, when they were in-

Temperance Hall High School is shown here during its last term in 1929–1930. Professor John F. Caplinger was the teacher; the pupils were George Lamberson, Clyde Foutch, Jessie Watson, Ruth Corley, Lizzie Tubb, Athaleen Corley, Delma Bates, Beulah Pittman, Wilma Midgett, Bartie Robinson, Corley Anderson, and Grace Close.

tegrated without major difficulty. Before the Civil War it was illegal to teach slaves to read or write, but black schools were established soon after the war. At one time there were black schools at Alexandria, Liberty, Temperance Hall, Wolf Creek, Smithville, and other locations in the county. Generally speaking, they were no better and no worse than the other schools in the county; although black teachers were paid less than white ones, neither black nor white schools had adequate equipment or supplies. It was difficult for black children to go to high school, but it was also difficult for white children. When school buses came into general use over the county in 1948, costs were paid for the fewer than 20 black students to ride the Trailway bus to attend high school in Lebanon.

High schools as we now know them did not exist in DeKalb County until about 1909, when the present school system was organized. In 1929 there were high schools at Alexandria, Blue Springs, Dowelltown, Dry Creek, Keltonburg, Laurel Hill, Liberty, Smithville, Snow's Hill, and Temperance Hall, some of which were two-year schools. Alexandria's high school remained into the 1940s, but lack of money during the Depression closed all of the others except the ones at Liberty and Smithville. These last two were consolidated into DeKalb County High School in 1963 after the high school building at Smithville burned. DeKalb County High School in 1984 had about 750 pupils and 40 teachers.

In the 1920s there was some consolidation of elementary schools, but during the Depression several of the schools re-opened. Finally, after World War II, the smaller schools gradually died out, until today there are only three elementary schools in DeKalb County: West Elementary at Liberty, and Smithville Elementary and DeKalb Middle School in Smithville.

The biggest problem for DeKalb County's schools in the past has been a lack of money. This has been alleviated to some extent by greater prosperity and by increased state funding of education. Today the county operates a school system which meets the needs of the majority of its pupils. A vocational school added to the high school campus in 1971 provides for the training of many students, while the regular school program gives adequate preparation for the 30 per cent of high school graduates who go on to college.

Religion

Churches were established early in DeKalb County and have been very important throughout its entire history. The county is and always was overwhelmingly Christian and Protestant; there are no Jewish congregations and only two small Catholic groups. About 90 per cent of the church members today are Baptist, Methodist, Presbyterian, or Church of Christ.

When the first churches were being established in DeKalb County around 1800 the Great Revival was sweeping through Kentucky and Tennessee. Church services at that time were marked by much "shouting" and other displays of emotion. Such behavior has now fallen into disfavor in most of the county's larger churches, but is still seen in many of the smaller churches and among some of the groups with fundamental beliefs.

Probably about two-thirds of DeKalb County's adult population are church members at the present time, though not all of these members attend church services regularly. A century and more ago just the reverse was true. Membership in the churches was much more limited than it is today, so that the number attending services was much larger than the number of members. Black slaves were readily accepted into membership. Salem Church had a black member, Samuel Forester, on its list of charter members in 1809, and continued to accept black members until after the Civil War, when the blacks organized their own churches. The Church of Christ at Smithville had black members until about 1910.

Even when a person was accepted as a church member, he might later be excluded. Members at Salem Baptist Church were excluded for such obvious things as "joining the Methodists" and "joining the Camolites." They were also excluded for fornication, for "the sin of drunkness," for slander, and for using profane language. In 1827 Hannah and Eliza Overall were excluded after holding a dance at their home. At Bildad Baptist Church in 1830 Sampson Cantrell was reported for "allowing frolicking at his house," while John Cantrell was accused of "shooting for beef at a shooting match," and Polly Tittle was excluded for fighting.

Church services are much more frequent today than they were before 1900. Most of the larger churches now have Sunday school every Sunday, worship service Sunday morning and Sunday night, Wednesday prayer service, various choir practices, meetings of young people, and so on. In the past century, most churches met only once a month except during the annual protracted meeting, which lasted a week or two. Many church and school buildings were used by several groups on different Sundays. The church at New Union, which is now The Baptist, was at one time used by four groups: The Baptist, Missionary Baptist, Methodist, and Cumberland Presbyterian. Until the 1930s the four groups held a joint revival every year.

The Baptist church was and is the largest denomination in DeKalb County. Of the nine churches in the county in 1820, five were Baptist; in 1980, about half the church members in the county were Baptists. The mother church of practically every Baptist church in DeKalb County is Salem Church at Liberty. Begun in 1804 as an arm of Brush Creek Church, it became an

Salem Baptist Church conducted this baptizing about 1912 just below the mill dam at Liberty. Since about half the churches in DeKalb County were Baptist, such scenes were common.

independent church in 1809 with William Bratten, Adam Dale, William Dale, Joseph Evans, and John Fite among the charter members. The organizer of Salem Church was Cantrell Bethel, who served as the first pastor, and as pastor at various times for the next 40 years. The same year he was instrumental in organizing Bildad Church near Keltonburg. Early members there included several of his brothers, his sister Constance Cantrell, and cousins and nephews such as Abraham Cantrell, Benjamin Cantrell, Perry Green Magness, and Tilman Potter.

Salem and Bildad churches are the oldest churches in the county; from them have come most of DeKalb County's present-day Baptist churches. In the 1830s and 1840s several of the Baptist churches divided over questions of doctrine. In 1980 more than half the county's Baptists were Missionary Baptists. The major groups among the remaining congregations are The Baptists, Freewill Baptists, and Primitive Baptists. The practice of foot-washing in some of these churches led them to be called "foot-washing Baptists." The best-known foot-washing was held at New Bildad Primitive Baptist Church on the second Sunday in May, and until the 1920s this event attracted enormous crowds, many of whom were not Baptists and many of whom never went near the church. There was preaching, all-day singing, and dinner on the ground; people came from as far away as McMinnville and Alexandria. One observer said that "Everybody who was anybody went; it was a bigger event than the county fair."

The second largest denomination in DeKalb County is the Methodist. They were known in the past century as "shouting Methodists" because of their emotional displays. Some of the Methodist churches had a straw pile in the corner, so that those who became exhausted from "shouting" could fall into it. Such displays have ceased, however, and the Methodists now are one of the most formal of the church groups. The oldest Methodist Church is at Alexandria; it dates to 1813. The Methodists were organized at Liberty by 1817. At both Smithville and Alexandria there were Methodist campgrounds in the 1840s. Families came in the late summer after crops were laid by and spent a week or two camping and attending preaching services two or three times a day. These camp meetings were very popular as social occasions, and were also much noted for displays of religious fervor.

Such displays were never a part of the services of the Church of Christ, or Christian Church, as it was known in the past century. The oldest Church of Christ congregation in DeKalb County has been active in Alexandria since 1835. A group was organized in 1852 at Sunny Point on Falling Water; this church was disbanded a century later when the area was covered by Center Hill Lake. Among the Church of Christ preachers active after the Civil War were Jeff Boles, Leo Boles, and J. M. Kidwell, who began the Church of Christ at Smithville in 1868 by preaching in the courthouse. In 1980 there were seven active Church of Christ congregations in DeKalb County.

Several of the very earliest settlers of DeKalb County were Presbyterians, including Adam Dale and Leonard Fite. In Tennessee, however, they became Baptists or Methodists, and there were few Presbyterians in DeKalb County. At Liberty in 1817 the Presbyterians shared a building with the Methodists, but the Presbyterian group was no longer active by the time of the Civil War. After that war, two Cumberland Presbyterian preachers were very active in DeKalb County. I. L. Thompson had churches at Banks and on Dry Creek; William G. Lewis preached in the Smithville area. While several Cumberland Presbyterian churches were established during this time, only three are now active: those at Jefferson, Banks, and Smithville.

The Baptist, Methodist, Cumberland Presbyterian, and Church of Christ groups had the only organized churches in DeKalb County for more than a century. However, beginning in the 1930s, a few other groups have been organized. These include the Pentecostal, Church of God, Emanuel Church of Christ, Catholic, Jehovah's Witnesses, Brethren in Christ, Church of the Nazarene, and Seventh-Day Adventists.

Most of the present-day churches in DeKalb County are relatively prosperous and have substantial buildings in which to hold their meetings. Though the churches have changed considerably over the years, and the attitude of people toward them has changed, there is probably more church activity in DeKalb County today than there has been at any time in the past.

Courts and Criminals

From earliest times DeKalb Countians have had disputes with each other, and there had to be courts of law to settle them. Conflicting claims and overlapping boundaries brought many landowners into court for settlement. Those who broke the law were also brought to court, and while all agreed that DeKalb County had its share of lawbreakers, some thought that it had even more than its share. Judge R. W. Smartt reported that DeKalb had "a very rough reputation" in 1918 when he became circuit judge for the five-county area which included DeKalb. Things were even worse in the 1890s when W. H. C. Lassiter was sheriff. Once, on his way to Mine Lick Creek to settle some trouble there, he met a big rough woman wielding a butcher knife in the road. She cursed mightily and asked if he had seen the sheriff, that she was looking for him. Mr. Lassiter told her that he had seen the sheriff on the road going to Falling Water, then rode on and left her still cursing in the road.

Both the criminals and those involved in property disputes required the services of judges and lawyers. Often the judges and lawyers were dramatic figures who could make a fine impression on juries and spectators. In the times before movies and television, court trials were a great form of entertainment, and lawyers were second only to preachers in their ability to make stirring and dramatic speeches. The weeks when circuit court was in session drew large crowds to the courthouse—jurors and witnesses were there, of course, but many men came just for the show. Elijah Whiteley sold homemade ginger cakes on the square, and the hotels did a booming business, as did the saloons before they were closed in 1877. After that, plenty of whiskey was still available in jugs hidden behind the livery stables.

Most of the lawyers lived in Smithville as it was the county seat; the records were kept there, and the courts met there. On occasion, there were lawyers in Alexandria, Liberty, and Dowelltown, but this was exceptional and still is; in 1984 the offices of all the DeKalb County attorneys are located in Smithville.

In earlier times the DeKalb County Quarterly Court had jurisdiction in certain cases. The justices of the peace who made up the court also served as judges in minor cases within their own districts. This jurisdiction ended when the General Sessions Court was established in 1949. A constitutional amendment in 1978 changed the county court to a county commission, and the justices of peace became county commissioners.

Property settlements, civil cases, and some divorces are handled by the Chancery Court, the presiding judge being known as the Chancellor. The Chancery Division covers several counties; the following DeKalb Countians have served as Chancellor: W. G. Crowley, W. W. Wade and his brother Tim Wade, and Bethel M. Webb.

Criminal cases are tried in the Circuit Court; its judge travels to several counties to hold court. With the exception of M. D. Smallman, the judge of the Circuit Court has generally come from one of the other counties of the circuit. Probably the best-known and most widely respected Circuit Court Judge was Bob Smartt of Warren County, who occupied the bench for 32 years, from 1918 to 1950. Moonshiners, chicken thieves, and murderers appeared before him, but he was always noted for his fair treatment of all. On occasion he even let a convicted man finish making his crop before starting a prison sentence. While Judge Smartt never resided in DeKalb County, in 1935 his daughter Ann married one of DeKalb County's aspiring young lawyers, Joe L. Evins.

Joe L. Evins in 1980 was one of DeKalb County's 14 practicing attorneys, with Douglas Hodges as his partner. However, the attorney with the longest DeKalb County practice is McAllen Foutch, a native of Alexandria, who began his law practice in 1938, and who served as Speaker of the House of Representatives in the Tennessee General Assembly from 1949 to 1953. Also in Mr. Foutch's office are three younger attorneys, Hilton Conger, Mike Corley (a native of Alexandria and 1980 law school graduate), and Vester Parsley. Other practicing attorneys in the county are Ramon M. Adcock, Frank Buck (who served several terms as Representative to the Tennessee General Assembly), Joe Carter, B. H. Cook, Jr., Stuart Dye, William F. Dyer, George LeFevre, and DeWitt Puckett.

There have been a number of outstanding lawyers over the years in DeKalb County, and it is not possible to name them all. In the period around the Civil War, William B. Stokes and John H. Savage were probably the two most eloquent speakers. Both served in the United States Congress and both were colonels in the Civil War, but they were usually on opposing sides, both in politics and in the courtroom. The same was true of John B. Robinson and Bethel M. Webb after the war; Bethel Webb was especially noted for being a dramatic orator. Alvin Avant, Bethel Cantrell and James NeSmith were other prominent attorneys of that era. Some of those practicing law in DeKalb County at the time of World War I were P. C. Crowley, Brown Davis, J. E. Drake, Dixie Floyd, J. A. Gothard, E. G. Lawson, David M. Robinson, and R. L. Turner, all of Smithville. Others were H. A. Bratten at

Liberty, James W. Parker at Alexandria, and W. B. Corley at Dowelltown.

No less interesting than the lawyers were their clients. They were charged with all sorts of crimes and misdemeanors; young men in particular were often charged with assault and battery, gambling, and disturbing public worship, though the latter is a charge that is now quite rare. On the other hand, divorce cases, which are now among the most frequently heard cases, were quite rare 150 years ago. They existed even then, however, and were not very different from today's. In 1856, a wife charged that her husband had cursed and abused her, had kicked her and shoved her out of the house, and "while sitting at the table for breakfast, had thrown a knife at her and cut her cheek." In 1830 a husband requested a divorce from his wife because she had run away to Illinois with another man, leaving her husband and their "three little children thus ruined and disgraced." The records do not give the final disposition of either divorce case.

In addition to such civil cases, there were criminal cases. In earliest times there were no prisons; criminals were punished by branding, whipping, or hanging. While most branding and whipping were eliminated before DeKalb became a county, public hanging was still practiced for many years, and DeKalb County had two legal hangings. The first took place in 1845 (after two trials and an appeal to the Tennessee Supreme Court), in the case of Jim, a slave who was convicted of killing another slave. Jim's owner, a Mr. Payne, had lived on Dry Creek, but moved from Tennessee to Alabama. He was in debt and attachments were issued for his property, including Jim. Jim ran away and returned to Dry Creek, where he had relatives among William Williams' slaves. Isaac, the slave of William Avant, had been hired to find out where Jim was and turn him in to the authorities. However, before he could do so, Isaac was shot and killed while sleeping on the floor of William William's kitchen on the night of January 14, 1843. Jim was convicted of his murder and was hanged before a large crowd a half mile north of Smithville.

The crowd at the Presswood hanging on May 24, 1872, was much larger and set the standards for a century to come. Every

An immense crowd filled the public square at Smithville to witness the hanging of 17-year-old John Presswood in 1872. Taken from the southwest corner of the square, this is the only known picture of DeKalb County's first courthouse.

political gathering at Smithville for the next 100 years was invariably described as "the biggest crowd since the Presswood hanging." It was a huge crowd for the time; about 8000 people were present, for there was much interest in the case of 17-year-old John Presswood. John had gone after midnight to the home of a neighbor, Jim Billings. Finding Jim gone down the Caney Fork on a rafting trip, John tried to force himself on Mrs. Billings. When she resisted, he hit her on the head with an ax and killed her. He also struck her 11-year-old daughter Inez and thought he had killed her; but she lived to tell the tale and to see him die at the end of a hangman's noose. Five days before his execution Presswood was baptized in Fall Creek by Green Magness, a Primitive Baptist preacher. On the day of the hanging he heard his funeral preached from the gallows to the vast crowd by Jerry W. Cullom, a Methodist preacher. After T. N. Christian read Presswood's confession to the crowd, Sheriff Henry Blackburn sprung the trap and young John Presswood paid with his life for the murder he had committed.

The only other hanging to take place in DeKalb County was not for murder; in fact, the hanging was considered murder.

Those involved in it were charged with murder, and they spent many months in jail. Twenty-four-year-old Charlie Davis of Shiney Rock was charged with the rape of 15-year-old Kate Hughes, a local girl whom he had escorted to a number of social events. When he was brought to the courthouse for a preliminary hearing on August 2, 1901, he was taken from the custody of Sheriff John T. Odom by a crowd of men led by the girl's father and cousins. Breaking away from them, Charlie almost escaped, but was overtaken by the mob and dragged a half mile south of town to a large oak tree. Here some men pleaded for his release, but others urged that he be hanged. The passions of the moment prevailed, and Charlie Davis died at the end of the rope. Eight men were charged with murder; most of them spent 18 months in jail before they were allowed to make bond. It was very difficult to find a jury to try the case. Finally in August 1906, five years after the event, two of the accused were brought to trial and found not guilty; the remaining cases were dismissed.

Another case at almost the same time involved murder in Sheriff Odom's own family. On July 4, 1903, the Cannon County sheriff with a group of his deputies surrounded a house near Jacob's Pillar Church. They demanded that Vance Wilson surrender to them, which he did with no resistance, 22 years to the day after he allegedly murdered his wife's father, Franklin Odom (the grandfather of Sheriff John Odom). On that 4th of July in 1881, Vance and his father-in-law had argued over a hired hand, and in the heat of the argument, Vance allegedly pulled out a pistol and shot and killed Mr. Odom. The event took place in Cannon County, but Vance Wilson was placed in the Rutherford County jail for safe-keeping because there was talk of lynching. On the night of December 11, 1881, a group of Vance's friends and relatives rode to the jail in Murfreesboro and broke him out. He was immediately placed in hiding, where he remained for the next 22 years. Most of this time was spent in DeKalb County, where his family moved soon after he left jail. In daytime he hid in the upstairs or in the barn; he sometimes got exercise by working in the garden by moonlight. At times he was moved to the home of other relatives, usually at night, but occasionally in day-

light disguised as a woman. His wife and children had to be care-
ful never to let a neighbor see anything suspicious. After 22 years
of this existence, Vance was finally recaptured. White-haired and
68 years old, Vance was placed for a while in the Nashville jail.
However, bond was made for him, and he returned home, where
in 1904 he died of natural causes, still unconvicted of the crime
of which he was accused.

Most criminal cases in 1980 are drug and alcohol offenses,
various forms of stealing, and worthless checks. Other criminal
behavior is relatively unusual, though there have been occasional murders, a number of which have remained unsolved to
the present time.

Spanish-American War and First World War

DeKalb County felt little effect from the Spanish-American
War, which began on April 28, 1898. Only four regiments of Tennessee volunteers were mustered into service and there was no
draft. Only a few DeKalb Countians fought in this war; probably
the best remembered is Elzie Givan of Liberty, who served two
years in the Phillipine Islands. He lived to be 96 years old and
even in his old age enjoyed giving a bugle call in his front yard.

The call to service in World War I did not come to DeKalb
Countians immediately, as this country did not enter the war at
its beginning. In fact, the outbreak of the war in Europe in 1914
aroused little interest in DeKalb County. The young men who
would be called into service were occupied with other matters.
In 1915 they organized a tennis club at Smithville; Alexandria
also had a tennis club. When fall came, the young people of both
towns had active possum hunting groups. Things were most
peaceful at Liberty, where on May Day evening Miss Macon Gothard planned a boat ride on Smith Fork. Under a full moon,
the group of young couples spent the evening "gently floating
up and down the stream." On the farms fodder pulling and
sorghum making were occupying the young men's time.

All this changed considerably when war was declared on April
6, 1917. Several of DeKalb's County's young men volunteered
for military service before the draft began in June. On Septem-

ber 5, 1917, the first draftees were seen off by large crowds at Smithville, Dowelltown, Liberty, and Alexandria. On September 26 nearly 4000 people gathered at Smithville as 57 draftees left for service; they were given a grand send-off with speeches, music, refreshments, and a Red Cross program. In May of 1918 the first 24 black draftees were honored with a banquet which included speeches by Dr. T. J. Potter of the DeKalb County draft board and Sidney Potter, a leader of the black community.

Several of the servicemen wrote letters which were published in the *Smithville Review*. Most of them were cheerful; Albert Estes in France wrote that he had "plenty to eat, a good place to sleep, and lots of good looking French girls to talk to." Most of the servicemen were homesick, as very few of the DeKalb Countians were placed in the same units, and they did not get to see any "homefolks" during their terms of service.

On the home front, a major effort was made to sell Liberty bonds and War Savings Stamps. Edgar Evins was chairman of the committee to sell War Savings Stamps and pushed DeKalb County over its quota. Firman Love presided over the sale of Liberty Bonds, and DeKalb County bought almost double its quota. The DeKalb War Savings $1000 club, of which Tom Webb was president, was a great aid in passing the quota. By August 1, 1918, there were 57 members who had bought at least $1000 in Liberty bonds.

When the war ended on November 11, 1918, there was great celebration in DeKalb County. The day was marked at Smithville with an automobile parade and ringing of bells; that night guns were fired, a bonfire was built on the square, and the streets were thronged with people. The servicemen also celebrated, for now they would be coming home. Some had been in only a short time; the last 36 men left only two weeks before the Armistice. Some would never return; the lives of 21 DeKalb Countians were lost in the war to make the world safe for democracy. They were Bob Adamson, James I. Beshears, Alvin Colwell, William H. Cripps, Dib Driver, Azle B. Floyd, James M. Foutch, John B. Hayes, William H. Holt, Perry H. Johnson, Aubry G. Judkins, Thomas H. Magness, Thomas J. Neal, Loice C. Page, Willie E. Puckett, Vester Smith, Rufus E. Tramel, Jasper W. Vanatta, Dallas C. Wagoner, Arthur Wester, Brown F. Windham.

Everyday Life Since World War I

The period between World War I and World War II brought a number of changes to DeKalb County. Probably the most striking of these was the installation of electric power in the four incorporated towns. It did not come to rural areas, however, until after World War II. At first this meant little more than a light bulb dangling on a cord from the middle of the ceiling, but eventually it brought refrigerators, radios, and phonographs. Even outside the towns things were brighter; improved Aladdin lamps gave a good light, and battery radios were in almost every DeKalb County home by the time World War II began.

Automobiles were not nearly as plentiful as radios, though their number did increase dramatically in the 1920s. Since most DeKalb Countians got their income from the farm, they were not as prosperous as many Americans were in the 1920s. Nevertheless almost 1000 cars were registerd in DeKalb County in 1930, three times as many as were registered in 1920. These cars were not without problems; flat tires were a common occurrence, and everyone expected to change tires on a journey of even a few miles. In 1926 Charles Dearman, Joe Evins, James Hooper, and T. B. Webb drove from Smithville to Nashville (driving time about 2½ hours); they had eight punctures on the return trip alone. They also had problems at the tollgate, as they had spent all their money in Nashville. After an hour's delay, they were finally allowed through the gate when they gave the gatekeeper a pair of socks and some other things they had bought in Nashville.

The growing number of automobiles was helpful to some DeKalb Countians. The flourishing automobile industry attracted them to leave their farms and seek the higher wages of Detroit's factories. A large number left DeKalb County and moved North to find jobs.

Some of those who stayed in DeKalb County were provided employment by Prohibition. When alcoholic beverages went off

Revenue agents were a constant danger to those who made whiskey. Shown here hauling off parts of an illegal DeKalb County still in the 1920s are Logan Malloy of McMinnville, W. B. Stone of Murfreesboro, and Garrison Robinson of Smithville.

the legal market DeKalb residents began to make whiskey for the illegal market. While some of the whiskey was consumed locally, most of it was sold to Nashville and Chattanooga bootleggers. Illegal stills operated in all parts of DeKalb County during the 1920s. It is difficult to say how many people were involved in this whiskey-making, but it has been estimated that in certain parts of the county, at least one family in three was making moonshine.

Other things were happening in the 1920s which were not illegal, but which many considered immoral. For example, women's fashions made a drastic change, with hems going up to or above the knee for the first time. This was coupled with liberal use of makeup and with women invading the men's barber shops to get their hair cut in the very short "bob" which was stylish then. Fast dances like the Charleston were popular. Many DeKalb Countians took to the new fashions; there was a Charleston contest at the Fourth of July celebration in Smithville. However, many others did not approve, and bobbed hair and short skirts were denounced in most of the churches.

Talking movies did not exist until 1929; but silent movies were shown in Smithville as early as 1919 at the Star Theater operated by Howard Windham, admission 15 cents. The Star Theater burned in 1922, but in 1928 Joe Evins opened the DeKalb Theater, which also showed silent movies. Sound was provided by Bill Jacobs at the player piano with a fine disregard for appropriate music: a love scene might be accompanied by "The Old Rugged Cross." Silent movies were also shown by Edgar Evins on a battery-operated projector at the one-room schools across the county, as well as at Liberty, Dowelltown, and Temperance Hall.

Besides these new inventions, there were other forms of recreation. Major league baseball was very popular throughout the nation, and sandlot baseball was popular on a local level in DeKalb County. Teams of young men formed in several communities, including Dry Creek, Walker's Chapel, Alexandria, and Dowelltown. There was intense rivalry among some of them, and Liberty and Smithville were particularly bitter rivals. About 1921 they agreed to play a five-game series to settle which town had the best team. Dr. J. T. Bell, Newt Johnson, and other citizens of Smithville contributed money to hire players from as far away as Kentucky. Liberty had also recruited players from Auburntown and Murfreesboro, but this did not keep them from strongly protesting when they lost to Smithville's team, which they pointed out had only two players who were actually from Smithville.

Less popular than baseball, but still generally accepted, was the revival of the Ku Klux Klan in the 1920s. Many of DeKalb County's most prominent citizens were members of the Klan. One black man at Smithville was warned to leave the county and did. Several whites who were engaged in what the Klan considered to be immoral conduct were also warned.

The Klan's activites faded as hard times came with the Great Depression, although DeKalb Countians did not suffer as people in the cities did. Little or no money was in circulation, but this was nothing new for most people in the county, as they had grown up with little cash. While much of the United States enjoyed prosperity in the 1920s, agricultural areas (including DeKalb County) were suffering from depressed prices. The local banks had already failed; two years before the stock market crash of 1929 brought bank failures all over the nation, two banks in Smithville and one in Alexandria had closed their doors. There was no federal deposit insurance then, so both depositors and stockholders suffered almost a total loss.

Many people left DeKalb County in the 1920s to find jobs in northern factories, but in the 1930s there were no jobs to be found anywhere. Landowners often had several young farmers wanting to rent their land for a share of the crop. Times were especially hard for young married couples, and many of them had to live for months or years with parents or other relatives. Money for shoes, clothes, school books, and such things was very hard to come by, and plenty of people did without some of these things. Food, however, could be grown at home, and very few people in DeKalb County went hungry even during the Depression. On the other hand, they bought very little at the store. They lived by the old saying: "Use it up, wear it out, make it do, do without." Not many new automobiles were bought in the 1930s; a wagon and team of mules furnished transportation for many families until after World War II. In the 1920s the school system had consolidated some schools and hired school wagons to transport pupils to them. The Depression ended that, and some of the one-teacher schools were reopened. At the same time, six of the nine high schools were closed as an economy measure.

As government programs were organized, DeKalb Countians worked with the WPA to build schools, improve roads, and build sanitary outdoor toilets. A number of young men also worked with the Civilian Conservation Corps, and in so doing traveled extensively outside the county. Many of them were destined to travel much more extensively when they were called into the armed services after the bombing of Pearl Harbor brought our country into World War II.

Politics, 1900–1980

Though the Civil War officially ended in 1865, it continued in some ways in DeKalb County for at least another century. The bitter divisions of the war were carried over into politics, and each election became a battle with the enemy. Anything was considered fair so long as it won the election, and people who were otherwise perfectly honest saw nothing wrong with fraudulent elections. Candidates had little choice but to buy votes; a certain number of votes were for sale, and if the candidate did not buy them, his opponent would. Voter registration was not required in Tennessee until 1951, and it was easy enough for one person to vote in two or three districts if the election officials were willing. They were usually willing if the voter was supporting the right slate of candidates. An even more effective method of changing election results was to stop the person carrying the ballot box from the rural districts to the county seat. Then the ballot box could be opened and the ballots removed and replaced with new ballots marked for the candidates of your choice.

Such practices were carried on in most counties in Tennessee and the South. Perhaps they were practiced more diligently in DeKalb County than elsewhere because the voters in DeKalb, unlike in many southern counties, have been about 40% Republican. On the national level, DeKalb County has generally supported Democratic candidates for president, but on the local level, a number of Republicans have been elected to county offices. Part of this was due to DeKalb's systems of nominating candidates. The Republican candidates were almost always selected by party delegates in a convention, while the Democratic candidates were usually selected in a countrywide primary. For various reasons, Republicans were allowed to vote in the Democratic primary, and they sometimes helped nominate the weakest candidate. At other times the Democrats would be so divided over the results of their primary that the losers would support the Republican nominee.

Until recent years elections for county officials, governors, state legislators, and U.S. congressmen were held every two years.

Presidents and senators were elected less often, but there was some kind of election going on most of the time, providing entertainment and excitement for all. On election day there was much whiskey-drinking and fighting, and as recently as June of 1980, in a Smithville city election, there were charges of buying votes with whiskey, accompanied by a fistfight in the courthouse yard.

Some elections were more memorable than others, although many were hard-fought affairs. Probably the closest and hardest fought of all was the election of 1922, when John E. Conger and George Puckett ran for the office of county court clerk. Mr. Conger was a Republican and had held the clerk's office for several terms. The Democrats, led by Tom Webb and Edgar Evins, made an all-out effort in 1922 to fill all courthouse positions with Democrats. The campaign was long and arduous; it was most vigorous in the districts around Smithville. The election was held in August, and when the results were counted, George Puckett had won over Mr. Conger by four votes. The Democrats held an all-night celebration in their pleasure at finally defeating John Conger. They celebrated a little too early, however; Mr. Conger challenged the election in court and successfully held the office another two years and four months.

Another memorable election took place in 1946 when Joe L. Evins made his first race for the United States Congress. DeKalb County's Republicans and Democrats were united in their efforts to send a DeKalb Countian to Congress for the first time since the Civil War era. There was no challenge to Republicans voting in the Democratic primary; in fact, there was little challenge to anyone voting. There was no voter registration then, and it was said that not only every man and woman in DeKalb County voted for Joe Evins, but so did many children and even some of the dead. At any rate, he performed his job so satisfactorily that he never again had a serious challenger in the 30 years he served as congressman. During his last years in Congress he served as chairman of the Small Business Committee. As an influential member of the House Appropriations Committee he was able to secure many federal projects for DeKalb County, including the

Joe L. Evins   McAllen Foutch

Model Cities program in the 1970s. There is little question that he had more influence on DeKalb County than any other one person in its entire history. He died in 1984, eight years after his retirement.

At about the same time that Joe Evins was being elected to national office, another DeKalb Countian was being elected to state office. McAllen Foutch, an Alexandria native, was not only elected DeKalb County's representative to the Tennessee General Assembly, but served as Speaker of the House of Representatives from 1949 to 1953. It was during this time that the old Lebanon-Sparta turnpike road was replaced by the new highway which is now Highway 70, primarily because of Mr. Foutch's influence. That highway was recently named in honor of him. He also served many years as chairman of the DeKalb County Democratic Party (resigning in 1974), as county attorney, and as city attorney for Smithville, Alexandria, Dowelltown, and Liberty. For many years he was the single most influential person in DeKalb County politics.

There have been great changes in county politics in recent years. While the political parties are still important, they are not as powerful as they were even a few years ago. Voter registration and voting machines have made it more difficult to buy votes or to change election results. Attempts have been made, of course; in 1958 the voter registration books were stolen just before the election and were never found. Then in 1974 a major attempt was made to avoid the voting machines, and more than 1000 absentee votes were made on paper ballots. However, the present election commission has ended many of these practices. In 1980 voting machines were in use in every precinct of the county. All county officials now serve terms of four years or more, so elections are held less often than they were, thus generating less interest in politics. One citizen summed up these changes by saying that elections are unquestionably more honest than they used to be, but they are also unquestionably less fun than they used to be.

Military Conflicts, 1941–1974

Though World War II had been going on in Europe for two years, it was not until Pearl Harbor was bombed on December 7, 1941, that the United States entered the war. That bombing united the people of the nation and the people of DeKalb County as few things had done before.

DeKalb Countians were called upon to sacrifice many things, and most of them willingly reduced their use of sugar, tires, and gasoline, among other items. Many families were called upon to make an even greater sacrifice: one or more of their sons. Even then, most families were willing, for they felt that the war was being fought to preserve the very life of our nation. Those who tried to evade the service were generally looked upon with contempt, a feeling that lasted for many years.

In World War II not only sons but daughters went into the armed services, and at least two DeKalb County women, Lou Frances Smith and Ruth Webb, volunteered for the WACs and WAVEs, doing office work so that men could be freed for combat duty. And many of the men from DeKalb County saw combat

Only five months after Pearl Harbor this group of DeKalb County men left to be inducted into the army. Pictured at six o'clock on the morning of April 13, 1942, are *first row:* Delton Walker, Tom Davis, Edward Hobson, Charles Turner, Leonard Ours, Lytle (Windy Bill) Whitlock, Ben Hancock, Otis Winnard, G. W. Puckett, Zeb Luna, and Roy Self. *On the second row:* Edward Lattimore, Walter R. Redmon, Firman Young, Henry Lee Hayes, Toy Parkerson, Sam Mullican, Houston Cantrell, Clyde Redmon, Wilse Knowles, unidentified, David Adamson, H. J. Judkins, unidentified, Carmack Willoughby, "Rooster" Adamson, and Bratten Malone.

duty. They served in every branch of the services, and in every theater of combat from the embattled beaches of the Pacific to the mine-strewn fields of Germany. Some met their deaths there. Some were captured and spent terrible years in German or Japanese prisons. Others were wounded and returned home scarred mentally and physically. Yet through it all, the people of DeKalb County remained united in the war effort.

With 700 or more DeKalb Countians involved in the war, almost every family in the county had a son, a nephew, or a neighbor in the service; listening to the war news on the radio became a daily ritual for most families. The mail was also very important; everyone waited eagerly to hear from those in service, while the servicemen were no less eager to get a letter from home telling about little sister graduating from eighth grade or about the cow having a new calf.

Several DeKalb Countians went North to work in the factories making military materials, but for those who stayed in DeKalb County, life went on about as usual. Gasoline was rationed; the ordinary user only got three gallons a week. This was not as much of a hardship as it might seem, however. Most people in town walked where they were going, and most people in the country still had horses and mules available. There were few tractors in the county, so farm production went on as usual. The rationing of canned goods was even less of a hardship, as most people in the county had their own gardens and canned and preserved most of their own food.

Civil defense units were organized and practice blackouts were held throughout the county. Aside from that and the men being away in service, there was little change in the pattern of life until 1943. In that year, the people living in DeKalb County got a glimpse of what war could be like.

In an effort to train soldiers for war in Europe, the Army held extended maneuvers in 21 counties of Middle Tennessee, including DeKalb County. Headquarters were set up at Cumberland University in Lebanon, and the trainees were divided into two opposing armies, the Red and the Blue. Each force probably had 100,000 or more men, along with tanks, trucks, artillery, and all other necessary equipment. Blank shells were fired in rifles and machine guns, but they made just as much noise as real ammunition. And the tanks tore down fences and damaged crops just as in a real war. The government paid for all damage, and there was little complaint among DeKalb County's people, for they felt that this was their small contribution to the war effort. During 1943 and 1944, when DeKalb County was in the "war zone," small groups of soldiers would be stationed at certain points throughout the county for a few days at a time. Nearby families always considered it a privilege to send them home-cooked meals during their stay. In an effort to entertain the servicemen, a USO was organized in a vacant store on the

Smithville's Fox Theater is shown here about 1942.

square in Smithville, and the Fox Theater opened for Sunday matinees, which it had never done before.

The end of the war, and in many ways the end of an era, came in 1945. The DeKalb Countians who were returning from service could come home with the satisfaction of a job well done. Some had sacrificed their health, and nearly thirty had sacrificed their lives, but they had defeated the forces which had set out to destroy their world. Now they could return to a changing DeKalb County to spend the postwar years in the most prosperous period the county had ever known.

Some veterans of World War II, however, were soon called back into service. When the Korean War broke out in 1950 members of the reserve were called back to active duty in the army, and several DeKalb Countians volunteered to serve in the navy, air force, and marines. Although some people questioned whether our country should be involved in the Korean War, there was enough patriotic feeling left from World War II that few people refused their call into the armed services.

This was not true, however, in the late 1960s when DeKalb County's young men were being called to serve in the Vietnam conflict. As the war dragged on with little real progress and with ever-mounting casualites, the people of DeKalb County became more and more dissatisfied. By 1968 many felt that their sons were being sacrificed needlessly and became divided in their feelings about the war. There were no antiwar demonstrations in DeKalb County, and there was still much evidence of patriotism. But as the fighting continued four more years, there grew a general distrust of our nation's leaders which still exists.

In tems of casualties, the Civil War remains by far the most terrible of the wars, with hundreds of DeKalb Countians killed and wounded. In a single Confederate company (Company A, 16th Infantry Regiment) 27 died, the same number of DeKalb Countians who died in all of World War II. Nevertheless, except for the Civil War, more DeKalb Countians were actively involved in the Second World War than in any other of our nation's wars.

Military casualties between 1941 and 1974 totaled 35 men. Those who died in service in World War II were: Alton W. Adamson, Danny Buterbaugh, Lee D. Cantrell, Jack B. Davis, James Dodd, Alton E. Ervin, Jakie E. Estes, Athel Lee Gill, Hoyte B. Granstaff, James C. Green, Daniel R. Hale, Fred D. House, Holly J. Howard, Chester C. Howell, Cody J. Johnson, Joe O. Johnson, Leon Johnson, John G. Magness, Orvel E. McDowell, Robert J. McGinness, Ivan B. Oakley, Garlon Ponder, Willie O. Putty, John K. Robinson, Harvie D. Taylor, James A. VanHooser, Thurman L. Young. William L. Evans gave his life in the police action in Korea; while Billy Anthony Adcock, Alvin Dale Hutchings, Gary G. Montgomery, L. B. Murphy, Ronnie E. Reeder, James C. Thomason, and Danny S. Young were casualties of the Vietnam conflict.

Postwar Life

The years following World War II brought to DeKalb County more change than it had ever seen before. Probably the biggest single change was brought about by the construction of Center Hill Dam. This Army Corps of Engineers project was planned to generate electricity, provide flood control, and provide fishing and other recreation. It was begun in 1942 as a part of the war

Upon completion of the dam in 1948, the land around the Caney Fork River and its tributaries was covered with the waters of Center Hill Lake. Fishing, swimming, and water skiing attract thousands of visitors to the lake each year.

effort. Patriotism was at a very high level, so the people who were most affected offered little opposition to the project. By the time the war was over most of them had accepted the idea that they had to leave their farms, homes, schools, and churches. A few, however, were bitterly opposed to moving and remained in their homes until the dam was completed and the water was literally in their front yards. Some in the Center Hill area relocated in DeKalb County, but many moved to other counties, and the county lost 4000 people between 1940 and 1950. Those who hoped to benefit from the increased tourist trade looked forward to the completion of the dam.

On November 27, 1948, the dam was closed, impounding the waters of Caney Fork River into Center Hill Lake, covering what had been farms and forests, and completely changing the face of the northern and eastern sections of DeKalb County. By 1951 the three power generating units (of 45,000 kilowatts each) were in operation; their electrical power was and is sold to TVA for distribution.

This helped to bring about another great change, the availability of electricity over the entire county. In August of 1940 the Caney Fork Electric Co-Operative was organized, but electricity did not become available to the rural areas of DeKalb County until after World War II. By 1961 all areas of the county were covered by electric service; and in 1980 less than a dozen residences were without electricity. Electricity brought with it refrigerators, freezers, electric cookstoves, and a source of constant entertainment—television.

Television was available in neither town nor country until 1947, so electricity and television came to the farm people at about the same time. The first people to get television found their homes filled with visitors every night, as the neighbors came to watch the new amusement. Soon, however, the neighbors got their own television sets, and visits became less frequent as more people spent their spare time watching television. In 1962 the Fox Theater in Smithville closed its doors, a victim of television and the drive-in movie. In 1980 cable television became available within the city limits of Smithville.

Television was new to DeKalb County, but the telephone had been around since 1882. At first, there was only one in each town; the earliest one in Smithville was in Brown Foster's store, while Alexandria's only telephone was in Johnny Garrison's store. Around 1900 small exchanges were organized in the towns; service was then extended into the rural areas, so that by World War I many parts of the county had telephone service. In 1951, however, much of this service was wrecked by a destructive ice storm. Then, through the efforts of Clay Avant of Alexandria and several other interested people, the DeKalb telephone cooperative was chartered in June of that year. It included Alexandria, Liberty, and Temperance Hall when it began operation in 1953. The Smithville exchange was added in 1954; today the entire county has private-line telephone service available.

Communication was further improved by the construction of radio station WJLE in Smithville. The station made its first broadcast on October 3, 1963, and has been under the management of Ralph Vaughn since 1971. Besides music and news, the station broadcasts such local events as church services, ball games, elections, and meetings of the school board and the county commission.

While electricity, telephones, and television brought great changes in the daily life of many DeKalb Countians, even greater changes were brought about by the development of large-scale industry in the county. Much of this industry was the manufacturing of clothing, employing many more women than men. This began in 1948 with the opening of the shirt factory in Smithville and has continued to the present time, when DeKalb County's industries still employ more women than men.

As people of the county became less dependent on farms for their living, some families left the rural areas and moved to town. In 1980 three times as many people lived in the towns as did in 1940; only about half as many people lived on farms in 1980 as did in 1940. Hollows on Dry Creek and Dismal Creek that were once occupied by a dozen families now have only two or three families. Where once there was a school with 100 pupils, the school bus now picks up six or eight pupils and takes them to a school several miles away.

A major change in the schools came in 1963 when black pupils and white pupils began attending the same schools. Most of DeKalb County's black citizens had already left the farms and owned homes in or near the towns. The black population had gradually decreased from 10 percent in 1860 to about 2 percent in 1980. Though there is still racial prejudice in DeKalb County, relations between blacks and whites are generally harmonious. Since the Civil Rights Act of 1965 there has been more social contact between blacks and whites, and there have been at least three interracial marriages.

DeKalb County's marriages, like those all over the nation, have been much less stable since World War II than they were in the preceding centuries. Divorce was rare 40 years ago; today it is commonplace. In 1979 there were 230 marriages and 104 divorces in DeKalb County. Perhaps one reason for the increase in divorce is the fact that many women now work outside the home and feel somewhat independent. Especially in the 1970s

DeKalb County women began to move into fields previously open only to men; we now have women service station operators and women bankers. Two young DeKalb County women, Donna Foster and Jenny Knowles, have recently graduated from medical school, while Sue Nixon Puckett is attending law school and will probably be DeKalb's first woman attorney.

Some major changes in DeKalb County came about through the Model Cities program. This was a federal program primarily designed to improve the quality of life in the nation's cities. However, Congressman Joe L. Evins, a member of the House Appropriations Committee, was able to convince his colleagues that it should be tried in at least one rural area, his native DeKalb County. Thus, beginning in 1967, several million dollars of federal money were poured into DeKalb County. Among the more tangible results of the program have been a new courthouse, city halls and community centers, a vocational school, the middle school, several parks, and the Smithville airport. The federal government has taken an increasingly prominent part in various ways in DeKalb County since World War II. Among the areas in which the government is involved are the Head Start and Follow Through projects in the school system, and housing projects for the elderly and low-income groups at Smithville, Liberty, Dowelltown, and Alexandria.

Many of these federal projects developed in the 1970s. Another change that occurred in the 1970s was a reversal of the trend for people to move from DeKalb County to the cities. Not only did more native DeKalb Countians remain at home, but a number of people moved into the county. Some were natives returning from Detroit and elsewhere, but some were people from such locations as New York, Florida, and California who were looking for a better place to live. Part of these newcomers left within a year or two, but some still make their homes in DeKalb County.

The people of DeKalb County today live very much as people do in other parts of the United States. They live in new brick three-bedroom houses, they have carpeted floors, they watch the same television programs, they eat pizza and spaghetti, and they drive their cars to work at factories and stores. Their children play Little League baseball, wear blue jeans and T-shirts, and play their stereos loud enough to wake the dead.

And yet not all of the old DeKalb County characteristics are gone. Since the oil crisis of 1973 heating with wood-burning stoves has once again become popular. Raising a garden has also regained popularity as food prices have risen steadily. Many families still enjoy such local foods as turnip greens, whippoorwill peas, cornbread, and blackberry cobbler. Smithville has a municipal swimming pool, but swimming holes in the creeks are still in use. Many people engage in the sports of hunting quail, doves, squirrels, and deer; fishing is also a popular sport. Most homes in DeKalb County have air-conditioning, yet many people still like to sit on their porches. Since about 1970 marijuana and other drugs have been in use in DeKalb County, along with the ever-popular alcohol; yet the churches of the county are strong and well-attended. Family reunions are more numerous than ever, even while the divorce rate rises. Ties between family and friends are still strong. At the time of death, the funeral homes are flooded with people bringing flowers, food, and sympathy to the bereaved family.

Televison and education have changed the speech of young DeKalb Countians, so that few of them have the strong rural accents that were once prevalent throughout the county. Yet the way native DeKalb Countians talk still has a southern hill flavor and is distinctly different from the way people talk in the North and West. In fact, DeKalb Countians are sufficiently independent that they think their manner of speaking is just as good as that of people anywhere. Most DeKalb Countians are great believers in the equality of all people, and they have steadfastly refused to believe themselves inferior to anyone. For this reason it has been difficult to establish any sort of social class system. There is not now, and there has never been, an exclusive upper class in DeKalb County. Probably we have all known each other and all of our backgrounds too well to permit any pretensions. There have always been those who had more money or property than others, but few efforts have been made to establish an aristocracy, and those few efforts have met with little success.

Most DeKalb Countians have had an excellent sense of humor, and have been able to laugh at their own and each other's weaknesses and failings. Social gatherings are much more likely to produce the sound of laughter than the sound of argument.

Neighbors are still willing to share with each other. One has more than enough tomatoes in the garden, another has extra bean seed, still another brings in a cake made by a new recipe. And when there is sickness, the neighbors still come to help feed the livestock and gather in the crops.

Some things are changing as more women go to public work. Now the old and sick often end their days in a nursing home, and the young begin their days with a baby-sitter. More meals are eaten in restaurants or at fast-food establishments, and even meals at home often are made of ready-cooked items from the store.

It is difficult to say what direction DeKalb County will take in the future. The trend since 1973 has been for DeKalb Countians to live more conservatively than they did in the 1950s and 1960s. They now buy less gasoline and travel less; they make their old cars last longer. They are building smaller houses; it is no longer standard practice to build both a living room and a family room. They raise more of their own food, and they cut wood to provide more of their own fuel. However, as rising prices continue to cut the buying power of each family, it has become more important for women to hold jobs, and it looks as if that trend will continue. Present evidence does not indicate that there will be rapid population growth in DeKalb County, or that there will be rapid industrial expansion. The rate of change was very fast between 1945 and 1975; it appears now to have slowed to some extent. However, events now unforeseen may change things in DeKalb County as much as did the Civil War or World War II. We know certainly that things will change, though we do not know certainly in what ways they will change.

The Towns

Life in the towns of DeKalb County has always been a little different from life in the country. There were poor people in the towns, and there were prosperous people in the country, but in the past it was generally felt that those who lived in town were more prosperous. They had more clothes, more leisure time, and more substantial houses. They seemed always to be a step ahead of those who lived in the country. They had frame houses rather than log houses; by the time people in the country got frame houses, people in town had electric lights. Certainly most people in town did less hard work than did farm families. Until about 1950 most town families had a garden, chickens, and possibly a cow or pig. But they did not have fodder-pulling, pea-picking, hay-hauling, tobacco-cutting, plowing, and all the other back-breaking jobs which farm families had. Time, industrial jobs, and the Caney Fork Electric Co-Op have changed all this. People in the country now have electricity, bathrooms, new brick houses, and everything people in town have, without the disadvantage of being crowded together.

In 1980 nearly half the population of DeKalb County lived in the four incorporated towns, but this was most certainly not the way things were in the past. As late as 1940 less than 15 percent of DeKalb County's people lived in the incorporated towns. The number was even smaller in earlier times, when practically everyone lived on the farm, and the towns existed primarily to serve those who lived on farms.

The earliest town, of course, was Liberty, founded by Adam Dale, DeKalb County's first settler, whose mill was the first business to be established there. He named the settlement in honor of the ideal for which he and his father had fought in the American Revolution. Adam Dale chose the town's location wisely; it is surrounded by fertile farmland and lofty hills, and though Smith Fork flows on three sides of it, Liberty is on high ground and has never been bothered by flood waters. By 1807 the town site had been laid off and divided into more than 50 half-acre lots. The streets were given women's names, with Sarah Street as the main commercial street, along which the turnpike eventually ran. Business grew rapidly; a tanyard was established on the north side of town by 1808, and a few years later another tanyard was established on the south side of town. By 1811 Isaac Dale was granted a license to operate a tavern; Dr. William P. Lawrence bought two lots in 1812, and Anthony Walke was established as the first merchant by 1817.

By 1850 Liberty had three merchants, two doctors, two saddlers, two cabinetmakers, two tailors, and a shoemaker. A livery stable and a drugstore were among later businesses of the town. The highway built in 1952 bypassed the old business section, and most of the present businesses are located on the highway. Liberty's 1980 population was 364; it has grown comparatively little over the years, and remains a small town with many of its old buildings still standing. In the past, Liberty attracted trade from a wide area, and its residents were prosperous. They built substantial houses and stores, and there are several residences that have been continuously occupied since before the Civil War.

There have been many changes in Liberty as old families died out and moved away, and new families moved in from the surrounding rural areas. Nevertheless many of today's residents are descended from the people who first settled the town; the present mayor, Edward Hale, is a descendant of Sophia Dale Givan, a sister of Liberty's founder, Adam Dale.

The founder of Alexandria, DeKalb County's second oldest town, was Daniel Alexander, who named the town for himself. Born in Maryland in 1773, Daniel Alexander was almost certainly the first settler of Alexandria. He was located there by 1801 and the next year was granted license to keep a tavern at his home, a two-story log house which stood where Alton Close lived in 1980. A fine spring of water in the backyard is still running clear and cold after almost 200 years.

On April 15, 1820, Daniel Alexander laid off the town of Alexandria with 24 lots, each 66 feet wide by 165 feet long. The early business district was approximately where it is now. Alexandria grew rapidly; by 1850 it was the largest town in DeKalb County, as well as the wealthiest. This remained true until well

The square in Alexandria is thronged with people during the week of the DeKalb County Fair in 1918.

after 1900, and was due largely to the efforts of the early citizens of the town. Among the early leaders were J. M. Baird, William Floyd, James Goodner, and Dr. T. J. Sneed; they were equal to any present-day Chamber of Commerce in their drive to achieve things for their town. Alexandria citizens were leaders in establishing the Lebanon-Sparta Turnpike in 1838; in the 1850s they chartered two more turnpikes, one to Lancaster and one to Rome in Smith County. In the same decade they established two excellent schools, one for young men and one for young ladies. And not least in importance, in April of 1856 they organized the DeKalb County Agricultural and Mechanical Society, and in October of that year held the first DeKalb County Fair. The fair is still being held at Alexandria each year, and is for many citizens still one of the biggest events of the year. Probably the most successful years for the fair were those when it was under the ownership and operation of Mr. Rob Roy, one of Alexandria's leading citizens. The fair was begun primarily to promote agriculture and improve livestock, but the present emphasis is decidedly more on the carnivals, the rides, and the grandstand shows. From about 1890 until the 1930s, a separate fair was held for black citizens; today's fair is open to all races. The fair is usually held in August; in recent years the grandstand at the fairground has also been used for a big event in July. This is the Down-to-Earth All-Day

Dib Burks of Alexandria was the director of the black fair held there until about 1935. He was also in charge of all fireworks at the fairs in Alexandria, Lebanon, Carthage, Cookeville, and Celina, as well as at the Tennesse State Fair in Nashville.

Gospel Singing, which began in 1957 and was a joint project of the *Nashville Tennessean,* Elmer Hinton (a columnist for the paper), Clay Avant (mayor of Alexandria), and the Alexandria Lions Club.

Alexandria today has a shirt factory, two banks, a thriving business district, and seven churches. The population has gradually increased, and in 1980 the town had 686 residents. The oldest structure in Alexandria is a log house built in 1823 and now a part of the home of Mr. and Mrs. Charles Jennings. It stands on original lot 14 and was once the home of James Goodner, a prominent early businessman. Alexandria had several two-story frame houses built by its prosperous merchants; some are still standing, but a number have been destroyed by fire. Probably Alexandria's most disastrous fire occurred on December 13, 1906, when the Bell Hotel and twenty other buildings on the north side of Main Street were completely destroyed. After this fire the stores were rebuilt with their fronts some 50 feet farther back, creating the Alexandria square as it now is.

There was a public square at Smithville, of course, from the time the town was laid out in 1838. Smithville had no founder; it was decreed by the legislature as the county seat and placed near the center of the new county on 50 acres donated by Bernard Richardson. Ninety-two lots of varying sizes were surveyed, with the courthouse and public square in the center. The business section was located on or near the square, and this remained

The funeral of John Windham in 1902 was conducted by the Odd Fellows Lodge, with burial at the Kennedy Cemetery near Smithville. Mr. Windham's family are around the casket.

so until the 1950s, when some businesses located on Highway 70. Smithville drew its trade from a wide area, and its merchants were prosperous enough to build substantial homes. Several of these are still standing, the oldest being the home of Mrs. Baxter Rice on West Main Street. Once the home of William H. Magness, Smithville's wealthiest early merchant, this house is the only structure in the town built before the Civil War. Smithville was first incorporated in 1843. In that same year it was one of 20 sites considered by the General Assembly for a permanent state capital.

Like Alexandria, Smithville has suffered several disastrous fires, especially during the 1920s when fire destroyed much of the business district and the courthouse as well. Although Smithville was the county seat, it was for many years smaller than Alexandria, and certainly less prosperous. As late as 1940 Smithville had less than 1000 people. However, the building of factories and the increasing number of government jobs at the county seat has brought about considerable growth in the town. In 1980 the population of the town was 3824, nearly one third of DeKalb County's total population.

In the years before World War II, when the town was smaller

and more people lived on farms, Saturday was always a big day in Smithville. Farm families rode to town in cars or trucks, or in wagons pulled by mules, which were hitched behind Foster Brothers' store or David J. Atnip's store. The more fortunate children got a nickel to buy an ice cream cone at Webb's Drug Store or Trapp's Cafe, and maybe even a dime for admission to the afternoon show at the Fox Theatre—always a Western movie, with a serial and a comedy. Men stood around the courthouse talking about crops and politics; women talked about gardens and children. A political speech or a preacher on the courthouse steps might enliven the day. The stores were busy from early until late; closing time was not until nine or ten o'clock that night. All this has passed, however; now Saturday in Smithville is just an ordinary day, and the county offices are only open until noon.

In the past, court week at Smithville provided a certain amount of entertainment, but this did not really compare with the fair at Alexandria. However, in 1971, Berry Williams, a Pulaski native who had recently moved to Smithville, organized the Old-Time Fiddlers' Jamboree and Crafts Fair. This attracted large numbers of visitors to Smithville on the July 4th weekend; the Jamboree has become an annual affair with crowds estimated at 50,000. The contest features bluegrass music and is held in the open air on the public square. Very few DeKalb Countians have taken part in the contest; for most local residents the Jamboree is primarily a social occasion and a tourist attraction.

DeKalb County's three oldest towns were first incorporated many years ago: Smithville in 1843, Alexandria in 1848, and Liberty in 1850. These corporations were ended, however, shortly after the passage of the "Four-Mile Law" in 1877. This law provided that no saloon could be operated within four miles of a school except in incorporated towns, so the corporations were abolished in an effort to eliminate saloons. After statewide prohibition of alcohol was passed in 1909, the towns were reincorporated, Alexandria in 1913 with O. P. Barry as mayor, Smithville in 1919 with Firman Love as mayor, and Liberty in 1947 with B. H. Hale as mayor.

The only other incorporated town in the county is Dowell-

A large crowd views the performance at the Old-Time Fiddler's Jamboree in Smithville on July 4, 1981.

town, which was not incorporated until 1949; Shelton Chapman was its first mayor. The town in 1980 had a population of 340. Only a mile from Liberty, Dowellton did not develop until 1867, when W. Frank Dowell began to sell lots. A post office was established and named for Mr. Dowell. At about the same time, Allan Wright established a small woolen factory, Wingate T. Robinson built a gristmill at the Big Spring, and James Ashworth opened the first store. These things helped to attract residents to Dowelltown, a number of whom were Union veterans of the Civil War. Their pensions helped to contribute to the prosperity of the town, and meetings of the Grand Army of the Republic were held there as long as these veterans lived. Dowelltown has been damaged by floods at various times, but its most notable event was the tornado which struck the town on April 3, 1974. This tornado left a path of destruction in other parts of the county before touching down on the south side of Dowelltown near the shirt factory. It moved northward along the street to the post office, destroying eighteen residences, the school, stores, the bank, and the post office. There were some injuries, but no Dowell-town residents were killed in this disastrous storm. A million dollars in federal funds was spent in Dowelltown after the tornado, though those whose property was actually damaged received little direct benefit.

Besides the four incorporated towns in DeKalb County, there are two small unincorporated towns, Temperance Hall and Keltonburg. Each has a population of about 100 people, and both have grown very little for many years. Temperance Hall developed northwest of the large house which Nicholas Smith bought in 1842 from its builder, Samuel Caplinger. The house was built about 1821 and is presently the only building in DeKalb County to be listed on the National Register of Historic Places. The unique structure was Temperance Hall's first and most imposing residence. Another interesting building still standing in Temperance Hall is the one which gave its name to the town. Presently the home of Mr. and Mrs. Ernest Nixon and Mr. and Mrs. Ted Kyle, it has a room on the second floor which was used as a meeting place by the Sons of Temperance, who organized there in 1849. The building was later used as a hotel, and until recent years part of it was used as a store. With an excellent mill to attract business, the town developed a thriving trade, and in 1915 had an outstanding school, two churches, a resident doctor, and six business houses. Business has declined through the years, however, and in 1980 Ernest Nixon operated the only store.

Like Temperance Hall, Keltonburg's first business was a mill, built about 1875 by James Kelton, for whom the post office was named. Bethel Magness was a merchant there for many years; the last store closed about 1981. Keltonburg has a Methodist Church, a Church of Christ, and a Baptist Church; it once had a two-year high school and three stores. Like Temperance Hall, its business declined as people left the farms to move to cities and towns.

The Fine Arts

DeKalb Countians in general would not be considered patrons of the fine arts, yet in many ways, many of them are and have been. DeKalb Countians love music and have from the earliest times. There was always fiddle-playing, banjo-picking, and square dancing. Such music survived in some parts of the county until after World War II, by which time most of it disappeared in the wave of country music and rock and roll produced on radio and television.

Although many churches in early times were opposed to fiddling and dancing, both practices persisted for well over a century. There was no class distinction; both Congressman William B. Stokes and his brother-in-law Horace Overall were excellent fiddlers, as was Horace Overall's slave, Jeff. Bunk and Bill Shaw, former slaves, were always in demand to play the fiddle and banjo at dances around the Falling Water area of the Caney Fork. Dances were especially popular with young people; Ab Hooper of Hurricane Creek said that he would walk or ride for miles to get to one, and that he attended every one he heard of.

While the churches were opposed to some types of music, they encouraged other types, and hymns were very popular. Women sang them as they went about their work, and sang their babies to sleep with them. Most of the early churches had no instruments to accompany their hymns, but by the 1880s many had organs or pianos. The Church of Christ and some Baptist groups still sing their hymns without instrumental accompaniment. In the past 20 years more attention has been paid to church choirs, and several churches in the county now have excellent ones.

The first piano in the county is said to have been bought by Mr. William Floyd of Alexandria before the Civil War. William H. Magness of Smithville bought one for his daughters a few years later. By 1900 well-brought-up young ladies in town were expected to take piano lessons, an idea that persisted for many years. In Smithville Mrs. Omagh Foster taught music near the school from the 1920s through the 1940s. She had pupils in piano, saxophone, violin, accordion, and other instruments, as well as a rhythm band of younger pupils. Her recitals were a very popular annual event which filled the 600-seat high school auditorium to capacity.

In 1959 a marching band was begun at DeKalb County High School; it has grown and improved through the years. Now under the direction of Randy Rhody, it has 85 members in the marching band and nearly 200 in the total band program; its annual concerts draw a crowd of nearly 2000.

In the 1890s a group of about 20 men in Smithville formed a brass band which was active for 30 years; there was a bandstand on the square at Smithville until after World War I. They played on Sunday afternoons and for special occasions. Alexandria also had a brass band during this same period, and Liberty had both white and black bands.

Many DeKalb Countians enjoyed music; fewer of them enjoyed literature. There were to begin with very few books. Most homes had a Bible, a few doctors and lawyers had small libraries, but before the Civil War it would have been difficult to find anyone who owned more than 25 books. This situation lasted for many years; when Mrs. Lorene Conger moved to Smithville in 1912, she found few residents with any books. She borrowed old magazines from Mrs. Ruby Bell, but she "almost starved to death" for something to read. The schools had no libraries until high schools were established, and then libraries were very limited. There were no public libraries; the first one in DeKalb County was established in 1939 by the Smithville Study Club in an unfinished bathroom in the home of Mrs. Walter L. Burton. From that humble beginning it progressed to the present Justin Potter Library, a handsome structure built in 1967, which in 1980 had a collection of 14,000 volumes. The library was built with federal funds which were matched by the Justin and Valerie Potter Foundation of Nashville. The library was named for the late Justin Potter, both of whose parents were natives of Smithville. A branch of the Justin Potter Library was established in Alexandria in 1968, and there are bookmobile stops at homes and stores in various communities. There are also libraries in all four schools, with a combined total of about 25,000 books. Magazines and newspapers are readily available; there has been home delivery of the Nashville daily papers in the towns since around 1900.

Newspapers published in DeKalb County have always been weeklies, with the earliest one being published at Alexandria. Called the *Independent,* it was published by W. H. Mott shortly before the Civil War and ended during the war. Alexandria's most successful newspaper was the *Alexandria Times,* which began publication in 1894 and continued for more than 25 years; Mr. Rob Roy was its publisher and editor for much of that time. Liberty also had a newspaper; in 1886 Will A. Vick began publication of the *Liberty Herald* and continued it until 1900.

Several newspapers were published in succession in Smithville after the Civil War: the *Highland Sun,* the *Journal,* the *Index,* and the *Watchman and Critic.* Finally in 1892 Frank Wallace began publication of the *Smithville Review,* which is still being published. Its editor for many years was Eugene Hendon, who came to Smithville from Shelbyville in 1902 and continued as editor until his death in 1946. Bill Dyer of Silver Point was editor from 1947 until 1965; he is now a Smithville attorney. The *Review* in recent years was bought by the Morris chain of newspapers of Savannah, Georgia. The editor is Mrs. Dorothy Isbell Walker, a native of Martin, Tennessee, who came to the *Review* in 1965. The weekly columns written by correspondents from various communities are among the most popular features in the *Review.* Two of the most noted correspondents were Miss Mary Reams of Mechanicsville, who died several years ago, and Mrs. Ocia Carter of Temperance Hall, who was still active in 1984. Her unique style has endeared her to readers from near and far, and her column is the most-read part of the *Review.* The *Review* in 1980 had a circulation of 4000. Sporadic attempts have been made to establish other newspapers in the county, but these have met with limited success.

DeKalb County's only novelist, Ed Bell, got his first writing experience on the Smithville high school newspaper in the 1920s. He later became a professional newspaperman in Murfreesboro. His first novel, *Fish on the Steeple,* was published in 1935.

DeKalb County's only novelist, Ed Bell, played on his high school basketball team when this picture was made in 1928.

In it, people and events in Smithville were so thinly disguised that they were easily recognizable, and it created quite a scandal at the time. Ed seldom returned to Smithville, and his second novel, *Tommy Lee Feathers*, was set in Murfreesboro, though he wrote several short stories with DeKalb County settings.

DeKalb County had few writers and even fewer painters. Mrs. Maggie Bethel Tubb of Alexandria painted an interesting portrait of her four-year-old daughter Livvie in the 1890s, and around 1900 a traveling artist gave lessons in Smithville to several people, including Mrs. Ruby Bell, Mrs. Nora Allen, and Mrs. Mattie Foster. These ladies produced several paintings, mainly of the romantic scenery popular at the time. At the present time, there are several painters; some have studied art in school, and others have taken private lessons. Most DeKalb Countians have a very definitely traditional taste in painting; no abstract work is seen at the occasional art shows that have been held. Among those exhibiting several paintings in recent shows were: Mrs. Guylene Atnip, Mrs. Elizabeth Lafever, Mrs. Carolyn Mullinax, Brian Robinson, Mrs. Betty Turner, and Mac Willoughby. Mrs. Charles

Jennings of Alexandria has taught art in some of the schools, and Mrs. Walteen Parker presently teaches art at DeKalb County High School.

The Joe L. Evins Arts and Crafts Center was built on Center Hill Lake in 1979 with federal funds to serve the entire Appalachian region. It has so far had little impact on the local scene.

Contributions

DeKalb County has contributed much to the state and nation. Since the earliest settlement it has sent soldiers and sailors to fight in the nation's wars. Many of these men served in the first line of action, and many lost their health; some lost their lives.

Two DeKalb Countians who served in the Civil War also served in the United States Congress. John H. Savage was a congressman in the 1850s, while William B. Stokes served in the difficult years just before and just after the Civil War. It was Stokes, a southerner and former slave-owner, who introduced into Congress the Fifteenth Amendment, which gave the former slaves the right to vote.

The only other congressman from DeKalb County was Joe L. Evins, a World War II veteran, who in 1946 was elected to the first of 15 terms in office. He served during the prosperous years following World War II and reached a position of considerable influence on the Appropriations Committee. This position enabled him to get large amounts of federal money spent on projects in DeKalb County and the Fourth Congressional District, especially during President Johnson's Great Society programs.

On the state level, DeKalb County has produced a number of influential leaders. Among several important state senators and legislators, probably the most outstanding was McAllen Foutch, who served as Speaker of the House of Representatives from 1949 to 1953. Two DeKalb Countians have tried for the governor's office. William B. Stokes in 1869 ran as a Radical Republican but was defeated; in 1916 John W. Overall of Liberty also ran as a Republican and was also defeated.

The business world has also drawn from DeKalb County. Bird S. Rhea and his son Isaac T. Rhea went into the steamboat business after the Civil War and moved to Nashville, where they later expanded into the grain business. Around 1910 Charlie Wilson of Smithville went into the milling business in Nashville, making Polly Rich flour. Martha White flour was also manufactured by a former DeKalb Countian, Cohen Williams of Dowelltown. Edward Potter, Sr., of Smithville became prominent in banking in Nashville; his son Edward, Jr., was the leader of Commerce Union Bank from 1916 until his death in 1976. Another son, Justin Potter, was involved in mining and other businesses.

In recent years, DeKalb County's college graduates have become biologists, engineers, nuclear physicists, and college professors, though most of them have had to leave the county to follow such occupations. Many DeKalb Countians have become prominent in one way or another, and have contributed much to the growth and welfare of the state and nation. Yet possibly the greatest contribution DeKalb County has made to the state and nation is not its prominent and important people, but its ordinary, everyday, working people. These are the people who have grown the nation's food and worked in its factories, who have had little education but plenty of common sense, who have been able to survive with little or no money, who have been the decent and hardworking citizens of which any nation might be proud.

Appendices

A. DeKalb County Officials

Sheriffs (the term of office was two years, with a limit of three consecutive terms, until 1978)

Pleasant A. Thomason 1838–1842
James McGuire 1842–1845
John Allen 1845–1848
John L. Dearman 1848–1852
Ezekiel W. Taylor, Sr., 1852–1856
John Donnell 1856–1858
J. Y. Stewart 1858–1860
John Hallum 1860–1862
Hezekiah Love 1862–1864
Wm. L. Hathaway 1865–1868
Charles J. Hill 1868–1870
James Henry Blackburn
    1870–1874
M. F. Doss 1874–1878
Charles S. Frazier 1878–1880
Ben M. Merritt 1880–1882
Charles S. Frazier 1882–1884
Houston S. Gill 1884–1888
Wm. H. C. Lassiter 1888–1892
Silas F. Anderson 1892–1896
Ben M. Merritt 1896–1898
Louis Merritt 1898
John T. Odom 1898–1902
Barnabas Taylor 1902–1904

L. Everett Love 1904–1908
George C. Puckett 1908–1912
Amon B. Frazier 1912–1916
George C. Puckett 1916–1920
Amon B. Frazier 1920–1922
J. Harlie Cantrell 1922–1926
Fred E. Terry 1926–1930
Albert F. Foutch 1930–1932
Charlie D. Eller 1932– 1934
John C. (Chub) Hill 1934–1938
Will Vickers 1938–1940
Alex O. Parker 1940–1942
John C. (Chub) Hill 1942–1946
Will Bullard 1946–1948
C. H. Malone 1948–1954
James Keith 1954–1958
Harrison Puckett 1958–1960
Harold Frazier 1960–1964
W. H. Bing 1964–1966
Doris Bing 1966
Will Hall Windham 1966–1970
Kelly Walker 1970–1972
Creston Bain 1972–1976
Dwight Mathis 1976–

Quarterly Court Judges (The term of office is eight years. Because of variations in state law there was sometimes a county judge and sometimes a chairman of the court in the years between 1838 and 1894. After 1894 the judge was elected by popular vote. In 1978 the office was changed to County Executive with a four-year term.)

Wm. H. Magness 1856–1864
Jesse T. Hollis 1872–1880
Wingate T. Robinson 1880–1884?
Martin L. Bonham 1894–1902
Robert C. Nesmith 1902–1905
James E. Drake 1905–1910
James B. Moore 1910–1918

James E. Drake 1918–1931
Kate Drake 1931–1934
Will H. Atwell 1934–1950
Homer Murphy 1950–1958
Harry Foutch 1958–1966
Billy J. Lafever 1966–1982
Keith Garrett 1982–

Trustees (the term of office was two years until 1962)

Wm. A. Pratt 1838–1840
Thomas Simpson 1840–1844
Milton Ward 1844–1848
Wm. H. Whaley 1848–1850
Barnabas L. Johnson 1850–1854
James Terry Trapp 1854–1858
David Fite 1858–1860
Joseph Banks 1860–1862
W. A. Nesmith 1862–1864
Milton Ward 1864–1866
John Griffith 1866–1870
Benjamin Cantrell 1870–1872
Brackett Estes 1872–1876
W. P. Smith 1876–1878
James H. Fite 1878–1880
James H. Fuson 1880–1882
J. W. Vantrease 1882–1884
H. Clay Eastham 1884–1886
T. D. Oakley 1886–1888
W. G. Evans 1888–1892
James A. Newby 1892–1894
J. W. Reynolds 1894–1898
H. Lee Overall 1898–1902
L. Poper Potter 1902–1904
Wm. N. Adcock 1904–1906
J. E. Hobson 1906–1908
James A. Phillips 1908–1910
W. L. Taylor 1910–1912

M. Thomas Cripps 1912–1914
Matt C. Bratten 1914–1916
W. F. Malone 1916–1918
Matt C. Bratten 1918–1920
S. L. Fitts 1920–1922
C. D. Williams 1922–1924
W. J. (Bill) Lafever 1924–1926
Floyd Young 1926–1928
Wilson L. Hobson 1928–1930
T. W. Adcock 1930–1932
J. N. (Poley) Gill 1932–1934
T. R. Foutch 1934–1936
W. R. Oakley 1936–1938
Walter L. Burton 1938–1940
Athol J. Foster 1940–1942
Alvin F. Vanhooser 1942–1944
Arden R. Johnson 1944–1946
Jack C. Smith 1946–1948
John Bill Evins 1948–1950
Jesse M. Washer 1950–1952
Aubrey Turner 1952–1954
Harry G. Foutch 1954–1956
Roberta Robinson 1956–1958
Jim Curtis 1958–1960
Charlie F. Johnson 1960–1962
Tom Moss 1962–1966
Charles Trapp 1966–1978
Ronnie Goodwin 1978–

Registers of Deeds (the term of office is four years)

Daniel Coggin 1838–1842
Washington J. Isbell 1842–1848
David Fite 1848–1856
Isaac Hill Hayes 1856–1860
John K. Bain 1860–1864
M. H. McNamer 1864–1868
Judson Dale 1868–1869
S. P. W. Maxwell 1869–1870
John C. Cannady 1870–1874
John B. Atwell 1874–1878
John Harrison 1878–1882
Ezekiel W. Taylor, Jr. 1882–1886
John G. Evans 1886–1889
Dabner M. Lockhart 1889–1894
David B. Worley 1894–1902

H. L. Foutch 1902–1906
E. G. Pedigo 1906–1914
W. H. Hays 1914–1918
L. G. Fuson 1918
Jess L. Hobson 1919–1922
Kate Stewart James 1922–1926
Lillie Mai Bain 1926–1938
Lucille Stewart 1938–1944
A. P. Hallum 1944–1946
Harold Frazier 1946–1950
George Waggoner 1950–1970
Evelyn Waggoner 1970
Wade Amonett 1970–1974
W. A. (Bill) Young 1974–

County Court Clerks (the term of office is four years)

Pleasant M. Wade 1838–1843
W.W. Wade 1844
Wm. B. Lawrence 1844–1848
Washington J. Isbell 1848–1859
Matthew T. Martin 1859–1863
Jesse T. Hollis, deputy 1863–1864
George W. Eastham 1864–1866
Perry Green Magness, Jr.
    1866–1874
Eli J. Evans 1874–1878
Zebulon P. Lee 1878–1886
H. K. Allen 1886–1890
Zebulon P. Lee 1890–1894

John E. Conger 1894–1898
W. Brown Foster 1898–1910
John E. Conger 1910–1924
James F. Roy 1924–1934
J. M. Young 1934–1938
Fred Tramel 1938–1946
Sam A . Love 1946–1954
J. Bernard Summers 1954–1962
Erbie Robinson 1962–1966
Delton Parsley 1966–1974
Jim Foutch 1974–1982
Catherine Newby 1982
David Foutch 1982–

Circuit Court Clerks (the term of office is four years)

David Fite 1838–1842
Monroe Tubb 1842–1843
Wm. J. Givan 1844–1845
David Fite 1845–1848
Wm. B. Lawrence 1848–1852
John B. Tubb 1852–1859
Jesse T. Hollis 1860–1866
W. T. Hoskins 1866–1868
Thomas N. Christian 1868–1880
T. W. Shields 1880–1894
James H. Fuson 1894–1898
Felix D. Helm 1898–1902
J. F. Foster 1902–1906

J. M. Young 1906–1910
Jack S. Allen 1910–1926
J. Fantley Trapp 1926–1934
Homer Murphy 1934–1942
Dixie Calhoun 1942–1946
T. B. Adams 1946–1950
James F. Roy 1950–1954
Hobson Reynolds 1954–1970
Virgil Johnson 1970–1972
Dean Estes 1972–1974
Frances Johnson Lockhart
    1974–1982
Caesar Dunn 1982–

Clerk and Master of Chancery Court (appointed by the chancellor)

Thomas Whaley 1845–1859
Washington J. Isbell 1859–1861
J. T. Hollis, deputy 1861–1866
Jesse T. Hollis 1866–1872
John B. Robinson 1872–1876
W. W. Wade 1876–1883
M. A. Crowley 1883–1892

Julius C. Webb 1892–1894
James B. Moore 1894–1907
Sam W. Foster 1907–1935
Bethel W. Foster 1935–1955
Sam A. Love 1955–1982
Gary Johnson 1982–1983
John Robert Nixon 1983–

General Sessions Judges (The term of office is eight years. The office was created in 1949 and assumed many of the functions of the justices of the peace.)

Richard R. Fredeking 1949
T. M. Yeargin 1950–1958
Charles G. White 1958–1966

James G. Ford, Jr. 1966–1982
Vester Parsley, Jr. 1982–

Superintendents of Schools (The term of office is four years. The superintendent was elected by the Quarterly Court until 1946, then by popular vote.)

James Terry Trapp 1871–1880
J. W. Overall 1880
Alvin Avant 1881–1887
A. J. (Dick) Goodson 1887–1889
M. T. (Trab) Martin 1889–1891
E. W. Brown 1891–1895
W. J. Gothard 1895–1899
James E. Drake 1899–1903
R. H. Lankford 1903–1907
Martha Robinson 1907–1909
John S. Woods 1909–1913
John F. Caplinger 1913–1917

Emmons D. Givan 1917–1918
Lucien L. McDowell 1918–1931
James Hooper 1931–1933
Clarence E. Braswell 1933–1937
M. M. (Roe) Harney 1937–1946
Grady Carter 1946–1950
M. M. (Roe) Harney 1950–1954
J. D. Hendrixson 1954–1966
Billy Rhody 1966–1970
J. D. Hendrixson 1970–1974
Elzie G. McBride 1974–1982
Aubrey Turner, Jr. 1982–

Tax Assessors (The term of office is four years. Prior to 1908 tax assessors were elected for each civil district.)

W. A. Huggins 1908–1924
Harmon Moore 1924–1928
R. L. (Buddy) Taylor 1928–1936
Walter W. Mason 1936–1944
Floyd V. Nixon 1944–1952
Herbert Hendrixson 1952–1964

W. Herman Stewart 1964–1968
Joe Cassity 1968–1972
Jim Fuson 1972–1980
Dale Staley 1980–1984
Jack Estes 1984–

Road Supervisors (first elected in 1944 for a four-year term)

Wilson Hobson 1944–1954
G. Lee Cantrell 1954–1963
Aubrey Turner 1963–1970

Jerry Malone 1970–1974
Lelon Thweatt 1974–1982
Donald Pack 1982–

B. DeKalb Countians in the Tennessee General Assembly

Senate

James McGuire (Dem.) 1847
Wm. B. Stokes (American) 1855
John F. Goodner (American) 1857
Wingate T. Robinson (Rep.) 1865
John A. Fuson (Rep.) 1867
Joseph Clarke (Unionist) 1872
Montreville D. Smallman (Dem.)
  1881, 1883

Beauregard G. Adcock
  (Dem.) 1893
Pleasant C. Crowley (Dem.) 1903
Oliver E. Underhill (Dem.)
  1917, 1925
J. Edgar Evins (Dem.) 1935, 1945
McAllen Foutch (Dem.) 1955

House of Representatives

Daniel Coggin (Whig) 1843
John A. Fuson (Whig) 1845, 1847
Wm. B. Stokes (Whig) 1849, 1851
Horace A. Overall (Dem.) 1853
Manson M. Brien (American) 1855
Abram Monroe Savage (Dem.)
    1857 (died in office)
Robert Cantrell (Dem.) 1857
Joshua J. Ford (Dem.) 1859
William Floyd 1861
John A. Fuson (Rep.) 1865
Wingate T. Robinson (Rep.) 1867
W. Alonzo Dunlap (Rep.) 1869
James P. Doss (Dem.) 1871, 1872
Joshua J. Ford (Dem.) 1877
Horace A. Overall (Dem.) 1883
James M. Allen (Dem.) 1885, 1887
Martin L. Bonham (Dem.)
    1889, 1890
John H. Savage Knowles
    (Dem.) 1891
Henry C. Givan (Dem.) 1893
Samuel Wauford (Populist) 1895
Alexander Travis Phillips
    (Dem.) 1897
William T. Dozier (Dem.) 1899
Pleasant C. Crowley (Dem.) 1901
Lycurgus Driver (Dem.)
    1903, 1905
John H. Savage Knowles
    (Dem.) 1907

John E. Conger (Rep.) 1909
A. Nixon Cathcart (Dem.) 1911
Norman Ross Robinson
    (Rep.) 1913
Horace M. Evans (Dem.) 1915
James W. Parker (Rep.) 1917
Brown Davis (Dem.) 1919
William N. Adcock (Rep.) 1921
George S. Buckner (Dem.) 1923
Tom Ed Driver (Dem.) 1925, 1927
Thomas Henry Chapman
    (Rep.) 1929
Worth Crowley (Dem.) 1931
George C. Puckett (Dem.) 1933
Grady M. Allison (Rep.) 1935
Robert Nixon (Dem.) 1937
Ulysses C. Ervin (Dem.) 1939
Eugene Hendon (Dem.) 1941
McAllen Foutch (Dem.) 1943,
    1945, 1947, 1949, 1951, 1953;
    Speaker of the House
    1949–1953
Milns Thoburn Puckett (Dem.)
    1955
McAllen Foutch (Dem.) 1957
Ramon Maxie Adcock (Dem.)
    1959, 1961
M. T. Puckett (Dem.) 1963, 1965
Frank Buck (Dem.) 1973, 1975,
    1977, 1979, 1981, 1983

C. Churches

This partial list of congregations which have been active in the county includes location, approximate date of organization, and, where applicable, the approximate date when the church ceased to be active (corrections and additions are solicited).

Missionary Baptist Churches

Salem	Liberty	August 1809
Goshen	Dismal Creek	July 1821–Nov. 1837
Cooper's Chapel	Dismal Creek	1880
First Baptist	Smithville	25 Aug. 1844

Indian Creek	Hurricane Ridge, moved 1948 from Indian Creek	Nov. 1844
Mount Zion	2 mi. S. of Temperance Hall	30 June 1851
New Hope	2 mi. E. of Alexandria	1817
Dry Creek	Dry Creek (An earlier Baptist Church existed here in 1821)	29 Aug. 1886
Round Hill	Upper Dry Creek	1881, consolidated with Dry Creek 1889
Dowelltown	Dowelltown	29 July 1894
First Baptist	Locust St., Alexandria	22 Jan 1887
Snow Hill	Snow Hill	27 March 1897
Wharton Springs	3 mi. S. of Smithville	6 July 1889
Elizabeth Chapel	Allen Ferry Road, moved from Holmes Creek 1948	15 Oct 1901
Wolf Creek	Wolf Creek	1846
Beech Grove	Mouth of Holmes' Creek	1858–1905
Bethel	Began 1814 as Cove Hollow, moved about 1830 to Temperance Hall, moved about 1848 2 miles N. on Smith Fork, dissolved 1891.	
Cave Spring	Adamson Branch	17 Oct. 1901
Rock Castle	Falling Water	destroyed in 1902 flood
Antioch	Falling Water	1860?-1900?
Peoples	Lower Helton	about 1975
Gospel Lighthouse	Carter St., Smithville	about 1975
Caney Fork	Lower Mine Lick	1840s?-about 1900
Keltonburg	Keltonburg	1983
Dale Ridge	Dale Ridge	1949
Upper Helton	2 mi. S. of Alexandria	1950
Malone's Chapel	Walkers Creek	about 1890
Oak Hill	near Allen's Chapel	existed 1911
Mt. Hermon	Cross Roads	1904
New Home	Short Mt. Road	1932
West Main	Alexandria	1976
Covenant	Short Mt. St., Smithville	1975
Sink Creek	1 mi. W. of Hwy 56	about 1975
Calvary	W. Main St., Smithville	1964
Mt. Zion (black)	High Street, Alexandria	about 1894
Bethlehem Community	Dry Creek Rd., Smithville	about 1968
Temple Independent	Miller Rd., Smithville	3 Sept. 1967

Washer's Chapel	Ridge above Long Branch	about 1895–1924
Mt. Nebo	Jefferson	1885–1920?
Negro Baptist	Liberty	about 1880–1930s
Negro Baptist	Smithville, Jackson St.	about 1890–1930s
Mt. Pleasant	Johnson's Chapel	1915–1934
Faith Baptist	old Sparta Hwy, Smithville	1982

The Baptist Churches

New Union	Belk	by 1860
Cedar Grove (Goathouse)	near Hurricane Bridge	about 1890–1930s
Helton Creek	Lower Helton	by 1871
Mt. View	Young Bend	about 1880
Mt. Hope	Jefferson	1861?
Tabernacle	Braswell Lane, Smithville	1966
Indian Mound	Indian Mound	1884
Spring Street	Spring St., Smithville	about 1972
Mt. Moriah	Pea Ridge	1875

Freewill Baptist Churches

Center Hill	District 16	1884–1946
Good Hope	Dale Ridge	1881–1911
Johnson's Chapel	Johnson's Chapel	1898
New West Point	old Sparta Highway	1894
Pisgah	Short Mt. Road	1896
Taylor's Providence	Indian Mound	1923
First Freewill	Smithville	25 Oct. 1964
Old–Fashion Freewill	Blue Springs	1974

Two-Seed Predestinarian Baptist Churches

| Holmes' Creek | Holmes' Creek | by 1818–1946 |
| Old Bildad | Keltonburg | June 1809 |

Primitive Baptist Churches

New Bildad	Sink Creek	1854 (1809)
Mt. View	Young Bend, moved 1970 to Shiney Rock	Nov. 1867
Holmes' Creek	Holmes' Creek	about 1870–1900
Helton	Dry Branch	1886–1920?
Walkers Chapel (black)	High St., Alexandria	1882
Capling	Dale Ridge	1874–1920s
Alum Cave Ridge	Dry Creek	1867–1910?

Cumberland Presbyterian Churches

Banks	near Warren and Cannon cos.	by 1851
Jefferson	Jefferson	1878
Smithville	S. College St.	1873
Smithville Colored	Smith Road	1902–1930s
Peedee	Eagle Creek	1880?–1902
Laurel Hill (now Pentecostal)	2 miles E. of Sligo	1879–1960s
Alexandria	Locust St.	1881–1918
Liberty	Liberty	1817-by 1860
Alum Cave Ridge	Dry Creek	1867-about 1910

Methodist Churches

Alexandria	Alexandria	1813
Liberty	Liberty	1817
Dowelltown	Dowelltown	1877
Smithville	Church Street	1838
Second Creek	Second Creek	1820s?-1946
Bethel	Blue Springs	by 1859
Webb's Chapel	Highway 56 South	1945
Buckner's Chapel	Highway 56 North	by 1888
Keltonburg (Magness Chapel)	Keltonburg	1893
Jacob's Pillar	Jacob's Pillar Road	1857
Bright Hill	3 mi. SE of Smithville	by 1849
McNamer's Chapel	Indian Creek	by 1883–1946
Asbury	1 mi. E. of Dowelltown	1844–1933
Pisgah	Hannah's Branch	by 1852
Long Branch (Hopewell)	Long Branch	by 1854
Peeled Chestnut	DeKalb-White County line	before 1900
Snow Hill	Snow Hill	by 1884
Temperance Hall	Temperance Hall	1873
Carter's Chapel	Wolf Creek	1885–1950s
St. Matthew's Chapel (black)	Smith Road, Smithville	1888–1940s
Cantrell's Chapel	Big Hurricane Creek	1881–1920s
Sweet Gum Bottom	District 16	1883–1910?
New Union	Cocoanut Ridge	1867–1900?
Fuller's Chapel	Dismal Creek	1880
Bennett's	Dismal Creek	by 1834–1860s?
Dowelltown African	Dowelltown	about 1914
Faith Congregational	north of Dowelltown	12 Sept. 1969
Allen's Chapel	2 mi. N. of Smithville	1911

Liberty (black)	Liberty	by 1880
Clear Fork	Near Gassaway	by 1858–
Alexandria African	by Alexandria Cemetery	1869
Temperance Hall African	Temperance Hall	1880s–1956
Bain's Meeting House	Allen Bend	by 1845–by 1914

Churches of Christ

Sunny Point	Mouth of Falling Water	1852–1946
Phillipi	3 mi. N. of Smithville	about 1938
Corinth	Belk	1888
Temperance Hall	Temperance Hall	about 1904
Alexandria	W. Main St., Alexandria	1835
Smithville	Armory St., Smithville	1868
Smithville Northside (black)	Highway 56	about 1900
Liberty	behind school, Liberty	1895–1940s?
Young Bend	Young Bend	1896–1930s?
Keltonburg	Keltonburg	about 1900?
Mt. Olive	Hwy. 56, 6 mi. S. of Smithville	1870s–about 1914
Cherry Hill	District 8	existed about 1900

Pentecostal Churches

First United	Short Mt. St., Smithville	April 1947
Calvary United	Airport Rd., Smithville	about 1975
Laurel Hill United	2 mi. E. of Sligo	18 July 1969
Gospel Lighthouse	Smithville	by 1976

Emmanuel Churches of Christ

Martin's Chapel	near Crossroads	1930s
Temperance Hall	Temperance Hall	1956
Shiney Rock	Shiney Rock	about 1970

Other Churches

Church of the Nazarene	Dearman St., Smithville	Feb. 1963
Jehovah's Witnesses	Hwy. 70 W. of Smithville	1974
Church of God	Hwy 70, Smithville	1949
The Tabernacle (non-denominational now Church of Jesus Christ)	off Short Mt. Road	1937

Pomeroy Chapel	Old Sparta Rd. E. of	
Mennonite; became	Smithville	1934
Nazarene, then		1943
Brethren in Christ		1963
Negro Church	Williams Crossroads,	1880–1910?
	District 8	
Agape Community	Adamson Branch	1972
Orthodox Catholic		
St. Gregory's Mission	W. Main St., Smithville	1976
Roman Catholic		
Seventh-Day Adventist	old Sparta Rd.,	1979
	Smithville	
Church of God of	Bright Hill Rd.,	1980
Prophecy	Smithville	
First Assembly of God	Bryant St., Smithville	1982

D. Old Civil Districts

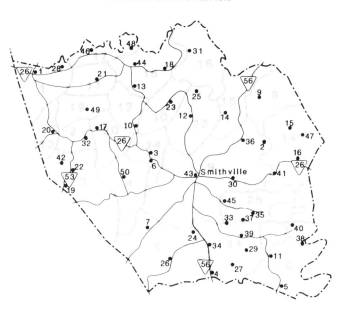

In 1969 seven districts of approximately equal population were created, and the number of justices of the peace was reduced from 54 to 14. The map above shows approximate boundaries of the old districts in 1939. The list on the next page gives the usual name of each district, its approximate date of creation, and the districts from which later ones were taken.

1. Alexandria, 1838
2. Liberty, 1838
3. Clear Fork and Pea Ridge 1838
4. Dry Creek, 1838
5. Blue Springs, 1838
6. Belk, 1838
7. Jefferson, 1838
8. Mine Lick (later Rock Castle), 1838
9. Smithville, 1838
10. Indian Creek (discontinued in 1948), 1838
11. Lower Helton, 1838
12. Hannah's Branch (from 11 & 2), 1840
13. Forks of the Pike (from 1 & 2), 1840
14. Falling Water and Johnson's Chapel (from 8), 1840
15. Temperance Hall (from 10 & Smith Co.), 1852
16. Wolf Creek (from Smith Co.), 1854
17. Walker's Creek (from Smith Co.), 1860
18. Second Creek (from 8 & 9), 1879
19. Dismal Creek (from 2 & 11), 1882
20. Dowelltown (from 2 & 4), 1887
21. Keltonburg (from 5, 6, & 7), 1888
22. Holmes' Creek (from 9 & 10, discontinued 1948), 1889
23. Indian Mound (from 7), 1905
24. Snow's Hill (from 9 & 20), 1910
25. Young Bend (from 7) 1917

E. DeKalb County Post Offices, 1808–1984

1. Alexandria 1821–present
2. Allen's Ferry 1830–about 1838
3. Atwell 1892–1895
4. Bear Branch 1874–1904
5. Belk 1893–1908
6. Blend 1901–1904?
7. Bluhms 1892–1904
8. Blyville 1889–1890 (not located)
9. Bozarth 1882–1909 (first known as Gibson's Landing 1878–1882
10. Capling 1885–1904
11. Catlens Mills 1872–1904
12. Citadel 1893–1904
13. Close 1890–1903
14. Crawfordton 1883–1904
15. DeKalb 1886–1904
16. Dillard 1904–1905
17. Dowelltown 1878–present
18. Exum 1890–1895, 1900–1904
19. Festoon 1890–1894
20. Forks of Pike 1879–1905
21. Foutch 1891–1903
22. Haleville 1888–1904
23. Hicks 1890–1904
24. Hollandsworth 1882–1904
25. Holmes Creek 1876–1897
26. Jones Mill 1878–1904
27. Joy 1894–1904
28. Kavenaugh 1807–1820??
29. Keltonburg 1884–1908
30. Kerley 3/1888–7/1888
31. Laurel Hill 1856–1905
32. Liberty 1808–present
33. Magness Mills 1878–1904
34. Mt. Sterling 1890–1904 (first known as Gladys 1889–1890)
35. Ozias 1880–1883
36. Pearlville 1902–1904
37. Pine Creek 1854–1860
38. Pinegar 1890–1904
39. Republican Grove 1848–1852
40. Shippingport 1833–1835
41. Sligo 1847–1853, 1859–1866
42. Smallman 1881–1890
43. Smithville 1838–present
44. Temperance Hall 1850–1904
45. Truth 1900–1904
46. Tubbville 1898–1904
47. Tyree's Mills 1853–1858
48. Vantreace 8/1883–9/1883
49. Whaley 1900–1903
50. Youngblood 1890–1904

F. DeKalb County Schools in 1904*

DISTRICT 1
1. Alexandria
2. Upper Helton
3. New Hope
4. Alexandria
   Colored
DISTRICT 2
5. Liberty
6. Liberty Colored
DISTRICT 3
7. Goggin House
8. Adamson Branch
9. Pea Ridge
10. Green Hill
11. Sweet Water
12. Buckeye College,
    Colored
DISTRICT 4
13. Possum Hollow
14. Dry Creek School
15. Mill School
16. George School
DISTRICT 5
17. Blue Springs
18. Mahathy Hill
19. Pillow (Watkins)
20. Oak Grove
21. Center Grove
22. Bluhm House
DISTRICT 6
23. Alexander
24. Gum Springs
25. Antioch
26. Savage Hill
DISTRICT 7
27. Mountain View
28. Jefferson
29. Indian Mound
30. New Hope

DISTRICT 8
31. Caney Fork
32. James House
33. Lafever House
34. Colored House
DISTRICT 9
35. Atwell House
36. Allen House
37. West Point
38. Walkers Chapel
39. Pure Fountain
    College
40. Bright Hill
41. Reynolds College
42. Cross Roads
43. Elliott Seminary
    Colored
44. League Chapel,
    Colored
DISTRICT 10
45. Cave Springs
46. Red Hill
DISTRICT 11
47. New Helton
DISTRICT 12
48. Pisgah
49. Williams House
DISTRICT 13
50. Four Corners
DISTRICT 14
51. Sunny Point
52. Rock Castle
53. New House
54. Laurel
55. Crowder House

DISTRICT 15
56. Temperance Hall
57. Close School
58. Cove Hollow
59. Long Branch
60. Temperance Hall
    Colored
DISTRICT 16
61. Coggin House
62. Center Hill
63. Colored House
64. Burton House
DISTRICT 17
65. Walkers Creek
66. Bethel
DISTRICT 18
67. Second Creek
68. New Union
69. Mud College
70. Atnip School
DISTRICT 19
71. Dismal Creek
DISTRICT 20
72. Eureka Academy
73. Bishop College,
    Colored
74. June Bug College
75. Snow Hill Colored
76. Capling
DISTRICT 21
77. Students Home
78. Bildad
79. Prosperity
DISTRICT 22
80. Chestnut Grove
81. Hurricane Creek
82. Holmes Creek
    (Pack)
83. Hale's Branch
84. Citadel

---

*taken from the Quarterly Court minutes of January 1, 1904

Suggested Reading

Bell, Ed. *Fish on the Steeple*. New York: Farrar & Rinehart, 1935.

Bell, Ed. *The Lonely People and Their Strange Ways*. Murfreesboro: Courier Printing, 1957.

Denny, Sam. *History of Long Branch*. The Author, 1975.

Douglas, Byrd. *Steamboatin' on the Cumberland*. Nashville: Tennessee Book, 1961.

Duke, Basil Wilson. *History of Morgan's Cavalry*. Cincinnati, 1867. Rpt. Indiana University Press, 1960.

Goodspeed Publishing Company. *A History of Tennessee from the Earliest Times to the Present, with Biographical Sketches of Cannon, Coffee, DeKalb, Warren, and White Counties*. Nashville, 1887. pp. 845–853 and 951–987.

Grime, John H. *History of Middle Tennessee Baptists*. Nashville, 1902.

Hale, William Thomas. *History of DeKalb County, Tennessee*. Nashville, 1915. Rpt. McMinnville: Ben Lomand, 1969.

Killebrew, Joseph B., et al. *Introduction to the Resources of Tennessee*. Nashville, 1874.

McDowell, Lucien L. *Songs of the Old Camp Ground: Genuine Religious Songs of the Tennessee Hill Country*. Ann Arbor, Mich.: Edwards Bros., 1937.

McDowell, Lucien L. and Flora Lassiter McDowell, comp. *Folk Dances of Tennessee: Folk Customs and Old Play Party Games of the Caney Fork Valley*. Ann Arbor, 1938. Rpt. Delaware, O.: Cooperative Research Service, 1953.

McDowell, Lucien L. and Flora Lassiter McDowell, comp. *Memory Melodies: A Collection of Folk Songs from Middle Tennessee*. Smithville, The Authors, 1947.

Nixon, W. H. *History of Indian Creek Baptist Church and Related Events*, 1965.

Owsley, Frank L. *Plain Folk of the Old South*. Baton Rouge: Louisiana State University Press, 1949.

Smith, Samuel D. and Stephen T. Rogers. *A Survey of Historic Pottery Making in Tennessee*. Division of Archaeology, Tennessee Department of Conservation, 1979.

Tennessee Civil War Centennial Commission. *Tennesseans in the Civil War:*

A Military History of Confederate and Union Units with Available Rosters of Personnel. 2 vols. Nashville: Civil War Centennial Commission, 1964–65.

Biographies and Genealogies

Adcock, Mrs. Jimmie. *Adcock Family and Allied Families.* Austin, Tx: Diversified Printing, 1979.

Bain, Ethel M. *The Bain Family: Ancestors and Descendants of Peter Bain of Tennessee, 1775–1980.* San Angelo, Tx: Newsfoto Publishing, 1980.

Christie, Susan Cantrill. *The Cantrill–Cantrell Genealogy.* Brooklyn, 1908.

Darrah, Marsha Young. "Political Career of Col. William B. Stokes of Tennessee." M.A. Thesis, Tennessee Technological University, 1968.

Evins, Joe L. *The Evins Family Genealogy: An Updated Study.* Smithville, TN: Bradley Printing, 1983.

Fisher, Margaret, and Betty Fisher Cox. *The Fisher Line.* Owensboro, KY: Cook & McDowell, 1980.

Fite, Elizabeth M. Stephenson. *The Biographical and Genealogical Records of the Fite Family in the United States.* New York, 1907.

Graves, Susan B. *Evins of Tennessee: Twenty-five Years in Congress.* New York: Popular Library, 1971.

Kiger, Wenzola R. *Overall Family,* 1978.

Lacey, Hubert Wesley. *The Goodner Family.* Dayton, OH: 1960.

Love, Jolee. *Love Letters.* 2 vols. Nashville: Ambrose Printing, 1979.

Love, Jolee. *Love's Valley.* Nashville: Ambrose Printing, 1954.

McBride, Robert M., and Dan M. Robison. *Biographical Directory of Members of the Tennessee General Assembly.* vol. 1, 1796–1861; vol. 2, 1861–1901. Nashville: Tennessee State Library and Archives and Tennessee Historical Commission, 1975, 1979.

Taylor, Ardis. *On the Taylor Trail: The Family History of William Taylor, Sr. (ca. 1740–1820's).* Gwinner, ND: 1980.

Newspapers

Justin Potter Library in Smithville and the Tennessee State Library in Nashville have on microfilm all available copies of the *Liberty Herald,* 1886–1901, the *Alexandria Times,* 1894–1918, and the *Smithville Review,* 1892 to the present. Most of the years before 1920 are incomplete; some have only scattered issues.

Index

Illustrations are indicated by an asterisk following the page number.

133

About The Author

Thomas Gray Webb was born July 30, 1931, in Smithville, Tennessee, and has spent most of his life in DeKalb County. He graduated from DeKalb County High School in 1949 and from George Peabody College in 1952, when he began teaching in the DeKalb County school system. He has taught in one- and two-teacher schools, in Smithville Elementary School, Liberty High School, and in DeKalb County High School, where he is presently employed. Mr. Webb spent two years in the army during the Korean War, after which he earned a Master's degree from Peabody College. He has also attended the University of Utah, Brigham Young University, Vanderbilt University, and the University of Tennessee. He has been historian of DeKalb County since 1964.

Mr. Webb and his wife, Audrey Turner Webb, live on a farm and raise hogs, cattle, chickens, and a large garden. They are members of the Cumberland Presbyterian Church.